I0408840

Editor-in-Chief and Founder:
  Lyndon H. LaRouche, Jr.
Editorial Board: *Lyndon H. LaRouche, Jr. , Helga
  Zepp-LaRouche, Robert Ingraham, Tony
  Papert, Gerald Rose, Dennis Small, Jeffrey
  Steinberg, William Wertz*
Co-Editors: *Robert Ingraham, Tony Papert*
Managing Editor: *Nancy Spannaus*
Technology: *Marsha Freeman*
Books: *Katherine Notley*
Ebooks: *Richard Burden*
Graphics: *Alan Yue*
Photos: *Stuart Lewis*
Circulation Manager: *Stanley Ezrol*

INTELLIGENCE DIRECTORS
Counterintelligence: *Jeffrey Steinberg, Michele
  Steinberg*
Economics: *John Hoefle, Marcia Merry Baker,
  Paul Gallagher*
History: *Anton Chaitkin*
Ibero-America: *Dennis Small*
Russia and Eastern Europe: *Rachel Douglas*
United States: *Debra Freeman*

INTERNATIONAL BUREAUS
Bogotá: *Miriam Redondo*
Berlin: *Rainer Apel*
Copenhagen: *Tom Gillesberg*
Houston: *Harley Schlanger*
Lima: *Sara Madueño*
Melbourne: *Robert Barwick*
Mexico City: *Gerardo Castilleja Chávez*
New Delhi: *Ramtanu Maitra*
Paris: *Christine Bierre*
Stockholm: *Ulf Sandmark*
United Nations, N.Y.C.: *Leni Rubinstein*
Washington, D.C.: *William Jones*
Wiesbaden: *Göran Haglund*

ON THE WEB
e-mail: eirns@larouchepub.com
www.larouchepub.com
www.executiveintelligencereview.com
www.larouchepub.com/eiw
Webmaster: *John Sigerson*
Assistant Webmaster: *George Hollis*
Editor, Arabic-language edition: *Hussein Askary*

EIR (ISSN 0273-6314) *is published weekly
(50 issues), by EIR News Service, Inc.,
P.O. Box 17390, Washington, D.C. 20041-0390.
(703) 777-9451 ext. 415*

European Headquarters: E.I.R. GmbH, Postfach
Bahnstrasse 9a, D-65205, Wiesbaden, Germany
Tel: 49-611-73650
Homepage: http://www.eirna.com
e-mail: eirna@eirna.com
Director: Georg Neudecker

Montreal, Canada: 514-461-1557

Denmark: EIR - Danmark, Sankt Knuds Vej 11,
basement left, DK-1903 Frederiksberg, Denmark.
Tel.: +45 35 43 60 40, Fax: +45 35 43 87 57. e-mail:
eirdk@hotmail.com.

Mexico City: EIR, Sor Juana Inés de la Cruz 242-2
Col. Agricultura C.P. 11360
Delegación M. Hidalgo, México D.F.
Tel. (5525) 5318-2301
eirmexico@gmail.com

Canada Post Publication Sales Agreement
#40683579

Postmaster: Send all address changes to *EIR*, P.O.
Box 17390, Washington, D.C. 20041-0390.

Signed articles in *EIR* represent the views of the
authors, and not necessarily those of the Editorial
Board.

Your New
Responsibilities

Pass Glass-Steagall Now!

Helga Zepp-LaRouche's addressed a nationwide call of LaRouche PAC activists on Jan. 29. Her remarks have been edited.

Helga Zepp-LaRouche: First of all, hello to everybody. I think everybody knows that with the election of Donald Trump, the world has completely changed. German Foreign Minister Steinmeier put a fine point on it, saying that the Trump election means the end of the entire order of the 20th Century.

It is very clear that the United States now has a choice: One is to continue with the "special relationship" with Great Britain, which was the basis for the unipolar world for the last 25 years, more or less, with a few exceptions of the Clinton years. And it is clear that the British would like to continue that, which is why Theresa May was the first foreign head of government to come and try to re-establish that special relationship, which would be very, very bad.

On the other side there is the clear perspective that the United States could enter the strategic alliance with Russia—and possibly China and India—which would create the basis to really move world politics into a completely new paradigm of collaboration of major nations to solve urgent problems like the economic crisis, the terrorism problem, and many other such problems.

Now, it is extremely clear from the first week of Trump's being in office, that he intends to follow through on all of his election promises. From my standpoint it is very important that—given the fact that the problems are so manifold—that people not get freaked out about this action and that action, but really concentrate on the two absolutely most crucial questions without which nothing else can be solved.

The first very, very crucial question is that Trump promised that he would improve the relationship with Russia, and that, for the sake of world peace, is the most important issue. Because if Hillary Clinton had carried out her policies in Syria, with the no-fly zones and the whole provocation against Russia in particular, we would have been on a short road to World War III.

So therefore, the fact that Donald Trump spoke yesterday with five world leaders—among them, President Putin of Russia, and that they apparently established a very good rapport—is of the highest strategic importance. If you look at what the White House and the Kremlin issued afterwards, this is really important, because "Trump asked to convey his wishes of happiness and prosperity to the Russian people, saying that the American people had warm feelings towards Russia and its citizens." http://en.kremlin.ru/events/president/news/53787

This is very, very important, and I think we should really understand that if the United States and Russia can fix their relations, then every other problem can potentially be tackled.

Obviously, the second most important issue is that Trump had also promised in the election campaign to reintroduce Glass-Steagall, because everybody knows that the world is still in absolute danger of a repetition of the crash of 2008, which this time would be much, much worse than even the collapse of Lehman Brothers and AIG in September 2008—for the very simple reason that the banks which are too big to fail have grown by 40% or even more, the derivatives have grown, and all the so-called instruments of the central banks have been used up, including quantitative easing, including the whole question of interventions such as bank bail-outs and helicopter money, all of which are in discussion.

As a result, the danger of the collapse of the banking system is an absolute threat hanging over the whole world.

Now, it is very clear that Wall Street obviously does not want Glass-Steagall, because it would, to say the minimum, diminish their power greatly—but it is an absolute precondition for fixing the situation. And Mr. LaRouche has not only talked about Glass-Steagall, but he has defined, on a scientific basis, the four basic laws which are absolutely crucial to be implemented to get the world out of this crisis, which are:

• Glass-Steagall, exactly as Franklin D. Roosevelt implemented it in 1933;

• A national bank in the tradition of Alexander Hamilton

• A credit system

• And then a crash program for high-technology fusion power and international space cooperation, as the absolutely necessary way to increase the productivity of the labor force which has collapsed.

Consider, in addition, that the life expectancy in the United States has gone *down* for the first time—this is the clearest indicator an economy has collapsed—that the life expectancy of the population is going down.

This is the purpose of this call, because unfortunately the designated Treasury Secretary Mnuchin, in a hearing with Maria Cantwell in the Senate, said he is not for Glass-Steagall in the form of FDR—this he said is a very old law—but he wants to have a "21st century" law because otherwise the markets would not have sufficient liquidity. That argument is wrong, because if you go to a National Bank in the tradition of Alexander Hamilton, and a credit system in the tradition of the American System of economy, that is exactly the system which will provide credit for productive investment.

Therefore, his argument is not relevant, and that appointment could be the Achilles' heel of the Trump Ad-

ministration if it's not corrected, because I think everybody has seen there is tremendous turmoil. There is a deployment by the very same British Empire which is trying to pin Trump down on the special relationship with Great Britain, but that does not prevent them from deploying Soros and the principle of "color revolution,"—the same thing which was deployed against Ukraine in 2004 with the Orange Revolution, or Georgia, or the Arab Spring—using essentially the same means of color revolution for regime change, this time against Trump.

So therefore, this is not a peaceful time; this is not a time when you can wait it out, but I think the fact that Trump has shown that he wants to carry out his election promises, is, indeed, very promising. But I think we need the kind of mobilization to make sure that this absolutely crucial flank of Glass-Steagall is not missed, because that could be the one thing which would really ruin the whole potential.

And let me just end with that. I think people in the United States have to be aware that the whole world looks at this Trump election with great hope—not the old *laissez faire* neo-liberals and the people who believe in confrontation with Russia and China—but a lot of people, in India, in Europe, are looking at the potential of the Trump Administration with great expectation and hope. This is a unique historical chance, so a lot depends on making it succeed.

The potential is there, with China's New Silk Road, which already is a new system of financial and economic cooperation on a "win-win" basis, in which over 70 nations are cooperating; the offer to the United States to have a Silk Road exactly fits with Trump's promise to invest $1 trillion into an infrastructure program in the United States and, therefore, launch a recovery. But it does require the original Glass-Steagall.

So I want to end it here, because this is really the gist of the situation, and I think we need all of you to really help and intervene.

Lyndon LaRouche: I emphasize this.

EDITORIAL

British Frantic To Destroy Trump

Jan. 31—The mass demonstrations against President Trump, and the 24/7 news coverage denouncing him, are not only hypocritical, but demonstrate that the British are becoming hysterical that they might potentially lose control of the United States. Since the death of Franklin Roosevelt, and especially since the British assassination of John F. Kennedy, the British system has taken firm hold in Washington. While Wall Street seized full control over the nation's economic policy, using British "free trade" to replace Hamiltonian directed credit, the British also used the United States as the "dumb giant" to wage colonial wars on behalf of London and Wall Street, from Vietnam to the perpetual wars against sovereign, peaceful nations in the Mideast under both Bush and Obama. This sustained the imperial division of the world into East vs. West, leading to Obama's final efforts to provoke a U.S./NATO war against Russia and China.

Now Donald Trump raises the possibility, however remote, of the overturn of the imperial system, with his statements which could imply:

• Establishing a partnership with Russia to defeat the terrorist scourge (itself a creation of the British and their controlled monarchy in Saudi Arabia),

• Ending the free-trade policies which saw the West shut down its own industries while exploiting cheap labor in the underdeveloped nations,

• Ending the anti-growth and anti-science hoax of global warming, and

• Promising to restore the American System of economics through Glass-Steagall to rebuild American industry, infrastructure, and scientific research.

It is far from certain that Trump will fulfill these indications, but the implied threat itself has sent chills through the blue blood of the British Monarchy.

Now, the British "Stop the War Coalition" is leading protests against the very person who campaigned for office against Obama's perpetual warfare! British agent George Soros is funding mass demonstrations against Trump in the United States for supposedly being anti-Muslim, while supporting Obama, who killed tens of thousands of Muslims and drove millions of Muslims out of their homes. Trump is de-

nounced as "anti-science" for rejecting the fruitcake Prince Charles and his environmental fantasies, and calling for renewed space exploration and real scientific research.

Maybe the most vulnerable Achilles heel of the new President, has been his choice of the anti-Glass-Steagall banker (and serial forecloser) Steven Mnuchin to be his Treasury Secretary. A mass mobilization by La-Rouche PAC supporters and others is under way to stop the Mnuchin confirmation, aimed at thrusting the Glass-Steagall issue into the forefront of the politically chaotic situation. Given Mnuchin's 15-year association with George Soros, Republicans should also understand why his confirmation must be stopped.

Will Americans and Europeans capitulate to the fascist concept that if an American leader were to oppose colonial wars and commit to industrial progress, that this would oppose "Western values?" For years, the Anglo-American oligarchy and their press whores have peddled the lie that Russian and Chinese "aggression" must be stopped to save "western values," when in fact Russia and China have taken the lead in fostering the historic but discarded values of Western civilization—providing security and prosperity for their own people, and, through the New Silk Road process, taking that security and prosperity to the rest of the world. The United States, meanwhile, has fallen into mass unemployment and underemployment, the collapse of manufacturing, an unprecedented drug epidemic, and profound cultural decadence—while under President Obama the nation has been in perpetual warfare, with Obama proudly drawing up a drone "kill list" on a weekly basis. Was this "Western values?"

The moment is pregnant with potentialities, for a new paradigm uniting the world's peoples in a new Renaissance, based on science and the best of each nation's Classical culture. This will not come from Donald Trump; but the fact that he questions some of the rules of the British Empire, and might work with Russia and potentially also with China for world development, provides the basis for the world to respond to the historic leadership of Lyndon LaRouche for a new, truly human world.

EIR Contents

www.larouchepub.com Volume 44, Number 5, February 3, 2017

*Cover
This Week*

I. Strategic Briefing

Mobilize for Victory, Now!

The following contains excerpted transcripts from three LaRouche PAC sponsored activities which took place on consecutive days from January 26-28. These events, and the included dialogues with participants, occurred within the context of LaRouche PAC's mobilization to achieve the early implementation of Glass-Steagall legislation and to block the nomination of Steven Mnuchin as the new U.S. Treasury Secretary. A featured component within these discussions is the nature of the treasonous role being played, at this time, by the financial speculator George Soros.

The featured speakers in these events were Paul Gallagher, Economics Editor of EIR; Jason Ross, a leader of the LaRouche PAC Science Team; and Diane Sare, the head of the LaRouche PAC Manhattan Project. Additional remarks are supplied by Dennis Speed, also of the Manhattan Project and a contributing editor of EIR.

I. Thursday: Paul Gallagher on the LaRouche PAC Nationwide Activists' Call

'Pass Glass Steagall; Block Mnuchin'

Dennis Speed: Good evening. I'm here to welcome you to our activists' conference call with our special guest, Economics Editor for *EIR* magazine, Paul Gallagher. We're one week into the new Trump administration. In this tumultuous time, we have to think about the principle of "national union." America was built by Alexander Hamilton with that thought, a single indivisible intent to beat the British Empire and its

Schiller Institute
Paul Gallagher

idea of mankind, replacing it with an idea of freedom for scientific discovery, invention and creation. The Presidency of the United States was designed by Hamilton and Washington and it was embedded in the Constitution's Preamble, which was the idea that you place the general welfare above all. Local interests and individual interests, the confederacy that had been there earlier was to be subordinated to a single federal union, and this has been the single emphasis of Lyndon LaRouche and his Manhattan Project for over the past two years.

Lyndon LaRouche's Four Laws, starting with Glass-Steagall's reinstatement, are the re-imposition of the *Constitution of the United States*. As I think everybody on this phone call knows, there has been a de-constitutionalization of the United States. This is a process that started actually from the time of the impeachment of Bill Clinton, and that impeachment process should have included actually the repeal of Glass-Steagall. So, instead of looking at it merely as an action that Clinton took, it should be seen as an action of the destruction of the Presidency, and that was being done by some of our erstwhile British cousins—the mad cousins, the Satanic cousins of Great Britain. This was an assault on the sovereign powers of the Presidential system and that is what we are going after now.

The Trump Presidency is an opportunity but it is not a solution. Now Glass-Steagall is ours to win. Now, we have a problem which LaRouche has directly referenced, which is this munchkin by the name of Mnuchin, this character who is being put forward—he is actually a former employee of the Soros Fund Management. He's supposed to become the Secretary of the Treasury or maybe it's the "Secretary of Treachery." He's our target at the present time. He's a nut case. He's unsusceptible to reason, and what we need to hear from the President of the United States is the famous words, "You're fired!" when it comes to Mnuchin before he even gets there.

The idea is we want to create a process—and this phone call is part of that—where over the period between now and February 28th, when the President will make his first statement to the Joint Session of Congress; by that time, we want to put Glass-Steagall and the reinstatement of Glass-Steagall fully on the agenda. And so the question is how we make that happy moment real. That's why we are here tonight. We're here to mobilize and activate ourselves around that idea.

Paul Gallagher: Let me talk about what LaRouche PAC is doing right now, a number of things, and I want to concentrate or focus on what Dennis just referred to, with regard to keeping Steven Mnuchin out of the Treasury Department and advancing the Glass-Steagall Act by doing that, which we have begun in an intense way this week.

We are pushing and awaiting introduction of Glass-Steagall legislation in both of the houses of Congress once this period of retreats and reorganizations and so forth, which is essentially ending at the end of this month. We're pushing very hard for the introduction of Glass-Steagall in both houses. We're not just waiting for it, we'll be on Capitol Hill again on this, this coming week and we won't be the only ones. We'll be going in parallel there with at least one group of other Democrats who are coming in from parts of the Midwest who were Bernie Sanders supporters in the last election and have hitched themselves to the mobilization for Glass-Steagall; they will be there, too, and at the same time, pushing for early introduction of legislation of a real Hamiltonian national bank for infrastructure and manufacturing, the introduction of that is also potentially close. We're organizing intensively for those things.

At the same time, we're about to, in the immediate weeks ahead, hold some more conferences in Europe on the expansion of the New Silk Road, the World Land-Bridge policy, coming from, in particular, China and the credit institutions of the BRICS.

There are a wave of replacement of governments, national elections, rejection of the European Union and the euro going on across Europe. They're going to continue to happen in the upcoming months, and bringing

Office of the President-elect

Stephen Mnuchin

in political parties and governments which have an entirely different view, which are pro-Russian, for example; that is, they are in favor of collaboration with Putin's Russia. And at the same time the tremendous effects of China's long-range New Silk Road/World Land-Bridge infrastructure development organizing, coming into and having real economic impact, particularly in some of the Central Asian and Eastern European countries and beginning to come into the European countries themselves, as a potential.

This is turning heads in Europe. You had for example today, one of the most senior political leaders in Italy (not a particularly good fellow, but, nonetheless, he has been for a long time one of Italy's senior leaders) got up and demanded that Europe should get rid of the sanctions on Russia before Trump does, so as to get into a position for this BRICS alliance to bring economic development and trade into a growing Europe again.

In that situation, it has been possible for these conferences to draw extremely high-level and wide attendance—diplomatic, business, and political circles, with Helga LaRouche leading them. We're going to continue to do those; and at the same time emphasize this drive in the United States. And we think that we can get both Glass-Steagall in quickly and hopefully Hamiltonian National Bank legislation in as well.

We're also going to be putting out very shortly a pamphlet for mass distribution on LaRouche's Four Laws, very fully developed, and illustrated with some really new technologic and economic conceptions, in showing what kinds of growth and progress are really possible, if LaRouche's Four Laws or four actions that have to be taken by Congress and President, if they're carried out.

And we have developments that are very important in this regard coming from the New Silk Road itself for the United States. For example, the head of two of the sovereign wealth funds of China whose name is Ding Xuedong—he made a speech two weeks ago in Hong Kong in which he said, "Look, we have a lot of United States Treasury securities" (the estimate is $100 billion or thereabouts); "They are very low return. We want to convert them into different kinds of investments in the United States, investments in a real infrastructure build, in the United States, of the sort that the government is now aiming towards. That's what we want to do."

This is one of many expressions from Chinese government publications and businessmen like that, that there is readiness from the Asian powers both to invest in a Hamiltonian national credit institution which will power this and also to contribute in the actual building, they being the champion infrastructure builders of the world now, especially China and Japan.

So, that also can be brought to bear on the situation which, as Dennis indicated in terms of what the policies of the United States are now going to be, is extremely, extremely fluid, and we're in a situation to change it.

Despite the extreme importance of mobilizing on Congress in this way, it's really what the President does on these matters which is likely to be decisive. So we are targeting the first speech which President Trump will be making to a Joint Session of Congress; that will be on February 28th. That is the target for the petitioning that we are doing all over the United States and online—easily found on our website [http://lpac.co/trumpsotu]—the petition calling on Trump to reiterate his promise of Glass-Steagall and propose it to Congress in that speech to the Joint Session on the 28th. *That would be decisive, should he do it.* That petition drive and the lobbying in Washington when we do these fly-ins and drive-ins—that is aimed at causing that to happen.

It is extremely urgent that we stop the nomination of Steven Mnuchin as Treasury Secretary. As people know, he flatly opposed Glass-Steagall in his confirmation hearing in spite of the fact that he was

George Soros 2002

George Soros

reminded by Senator Maria Cantwell that the President who had nominated him had proposed Glass-Steagall during the campaign. Nonetheless, Mnuchin opposed it with a completely phony argument. Many of the Democrats were opposing him anyway because of his practices of throwing tens of thousands of households out of their homes by foreclosure after he became the CEO of OneWest Bank, the successor of IndyMac Bank, which went bankrupt back in 2007.

More importantly, because we are dealing with the nation and the current Presidency and the current leadership of Congress, this Mnuchin is, for the last 15 years an employee, an investment partner, a business partner of George Soros, continuously during that period of time—Soros, who sponsored the state senatorial campaign of Barack Obama; Soros who sponsored the Federal senatorial campaign of Barack Obama; Soros who was the financial godfather, more than any other financial force, who made Obama's candidacy for the President in the first place in 2007 and 2008, and was an extraordinary force on and in the Obama administration; Soros without whom there has not been a single campaign in any state in the country for the legalization of drugs—every one of them backed and financed by his Open Society Institute and other Soros fronts—and that, in turn, having a profound influence on the pro-drug legalization position and policy of the Obama Justice Department.

This Soros who has immediately after the election

declared in Davos, in that meeting of millionaires and billionaires that takes place in the winter over there, in Switzerland, declares that he wanted the Trump administration to fail, that it would fail. He claimed that he was among those who were most desirous that it should fail, and who have already backed a completely meritless so-called Constitutional lawsuit trying to prove that Trump is violating the U.S. Constitution and should be impeached—a totally far-fetched lawsuit, but nonetheless one which has been brought into court by an outfit called CREW in Washington, D.C.—one of these NGO-type outfits which Soros is backing.

Yet, the standing nominee for Treasury Secretary right now is for the last fifteen years, initially an employee, then a business partner, and then a co-investor with Soros. In fact, this was rather blatantly ignored in the confirmation hearing for Mnuchin last week when many of the activities, illegal and/or immoral, of the OneWest Bank were being discussed by the Democrats on that panel. They kept referring to this as Mnuchin's bank, never mentioning the fact, which is widely known to everyone, that the consortium of hedge funds which took over IndyMac and made it into OneWest Bank was led by George Soros' hedge fund, Soros Fund Management; it was a coalition of six hedge funds headed by Soros' hedge fund and John Paulson's hedge fund, they are the ones who took IndyMac out of bankruptcy with a hell of a lot of money from the FDIC to help them out, a lot of bail-out; turned it into OneWest Bank and later made a bundle from it. Mnuchin was their CEO, but it was never mentioned that this was a Soros takeover of the bank. So, we had a confirmation hearing in which *the most salient fact* about the nominee was never mentioned by those who were discussing what the nominee had done under the influence of that salient factor, George Soros.

We put out a statement from Lyndon LaRouche on Monday and more recently this morning a leaflet, that has already gone out in many places demanding that the nomination must be stopped. [https://larouchepac.com/20170126/keep-george-soros-ally-steven-mnuchin-away-trump-treasury]. This guy must be kept out of the Treasury because as LaRouche said, "He will bring a deadly economic crash on the country if he's put in there."

In the hearing, Mnuchin made an argument against Glass-Steagall which is completely fallacious. He claimed that it would reduce the amount of bank lending in the country and would harm the capital markets if Glass-Steagall were restored. The exact opposite is the case, and we've just in fact had some graphic evidence of that just today published in *American Banker* magazine, so this whole hearing was a lie. Obviously, there is a lot of Democratic opposition to it, but this is a question for the Republicans on that panel, in particular, and a matter for Republican members of Congress of both houses, that, in effect, the *leading enemy of their administration* is the current nominee for Treasury, and they have to boot him out.

Question: The thing that you just brought out with the Soros connection of Mnuchin is the type of information, which is why LaRouche PAC is on the cutting edge of analyzing these situations. Another one is a guy named Cohn, who is coming out of Goldman Sachs. His deal, which was reported in the *Wall Street Journal* yesterday, is that they are rewarding him before he goes into the administration with a package worth $100 million, including $65 million in cash. It is virtually impossible for any individual to be objective or unbiased if he's coming into an administration with a gift of $65 million from the firm that he just came from. And his position is going to be as a leader of the National Economic Council. He's not going to be able to give unbiased advice in any way with that kind of a situation.

Gallagher: There's a flock of them from Wall Street, and the principle in this situation, something that Lyn has talked about many times over the past, is that you aim for the lead duck in the flock. When they're flying over, you don't just aim wildly at the whole flight, you aim for the lead duck.

And here, we're talking about a different duck than even these other Wall Street types like Gary Cohn. We're talking about a British agent who has been pushing for, and pushing effectively in many cases governments into place, in some countries particularly in Eastern Europe, and occasionally in Central and Western Europe, pushing governments into place on the principle that speculators should run things; that essentially the financial sector should be in charge of policy and the kind of speculation that Soros represents should be completely unfettered and deregulated.

He's intervened very strategically, as for example in the Barack Obama case, and a lot of Republicans know that. I can go all the way back to 2007, when Lyndon LaRouche designed what he called the Homeowners and Bank Protection Act in the early stages of the foreclosure crisis in 2006-2007, which was essentially an act which combined Glass-Steagall banking reorganization with a national foreclosure holiday or foreclosure moratorium, while that reorganization was taking place.

We were very close to the introduction of that legislation into Congress, by a congressman from Pennsylvania, and he received a call—he said so publicly in a press conference—he received a call directly from George Soros who told him that if this proposed legislation from LaRouche was introduced by him and were it to pass, that it would cause a complete collapse of the money market mutual funds and the financial markets generally. The congressman, as he said in his public statement, was not therefore going introduce LaRouche's legislation.

So a year later, precisely that crash—without the Homeowners and Bank Protection Act being introduced, or the Glass-Steagall principle in operation—that crash which Soros had falsely told the guy about, took place throughout the whole financial system. This is the kind of intervention that Soros does. And he's got a very targeted intervention, as he put it in Davos, to make sure that the Trump administration is a failure from the outset.

Mnuchin, as soon as he left Goldman Sachs fifteen years ago, was recruited by Soros to run the hedge fund backed by Soros called SFM Capital. It was created by Soros to buy risky assets; it was operated by Mnuchin. He then worked for Soros Funds Management; he then had Soros' backing to found Dune Capital Management, which is the one that he presented himself to the Senate as running; and then, as I indicated before, he became the CEO of a bank taken over by a coalition of hedge funds headed by Soros's hedge fund, and was put in to manage that OneWest Bank, aside from all of its dirty practices.

So Democrats are now holding that nomination up because of some of those dirty practices and other things. That is an opening, and the question is on the Republican side. And the worst enemy of the nation and of the current administration is the employer and partner of the nominee; so, will they stop it? And this is a question on which Republican offices, Republican members of Congress who have their staff in their offices around the country and their offices in Washington counting calls: how many came in for this guy, how many came in against? When we've been on the Hill

we've all seen this going on. The young people who sit there and take these calls, just count them.

So any network you can organize to target one of the members on that side, every one of those calls will be scratched down on the pad and counted. And this is really a critical window which has been opened by the fact that his nomination is being delayed because of the crimes the bank committed.

Question: We've recently had presentations on One Belt, One Road and on Chinese culture over the past few weeks, and the effect on those participants was very inspiring to see the work that was being done there. And I notice that people do respond to that, to help bring them into the Glass-Steagall concept around the AIIB and the initiative that China's doing, where the private sector has involvement, but not as a monopoly as such, but in design and construction phases for the projects that are needed here in the United States, and then, of course, we have an international flavor.

So can we talk a little bit more about how we organize around Glass-Steagall, where our citizens are brought into what Glass-Steagall really is, which is an international law that needs to be implemented globally?

Gallagher: It's going to be implemented globally one way or another. I mean, many people are not aware that there is and has been for the past twenty-four years a Glass-Steagall type of bank separation law in China. They've debated it over that time. There have been certain voices raised in the economics community in China, calling for doing away with it, and going to the universal bank model; but they have not succeeded, and the Chinese, both their so-called "policy banks," their state banks, and also the private commercial banks remain separated from the so-called "nonbank sector." And it makes a difference both in terms of lending capacity and also in terms of ability to absorb the effects of nonperforming loans in certain sectors of the economy.

Now, Trump said in his first European interview last week, that sent a lot of people through the ceiling over there, he said that he expected more countries to leave the euro. Today, his probable nominee for ambassador to the European Union repeated that, and said that he expected the European Union to break up over the next year and a half. This is actually something that a lot of the euro-skeptic forces who are pro-Glass-Steagall in Europe are waiting to see happen.

So it's politically interconnected. It's also, of course, a question that you've got to have commercial banking systems in the United States and the European countries, which are prepared to lend, whose business is lending and not securities speculation; and if that's the case, they will do that, and they will participate in a national credit flow which is going to building new infrastructure platforms and fostering manufacturing. The private commercial banks will participate in that to the fullest, if they are separated and insured under Glass-Steagall regulation. So it's both politically and economically interconnected in that way.

Question: I have a friend, and he wants to know about this "21st Century Glass-Steagall" talk, versus what FDR's Glass-Steagall actually was.

Gallagher: The "21st Century Glass-Steagall Act," ironically, is the name of the legislation in the Senate, the McCain-Warren-Cantwell-King bill. Their legislation was called the 21st Century Glass-Steagall Act. What that meant was that it was the Glass-Steagall Act with a new additional section which targeted derivatives. That new section said: "Here, we are redefining those activities which are not sufficiently close to banking as to be considered an essential part of it, and therefore are not permitted to commercial banks." And that section is primarily devoted to defining derivatives, not just derivatives speculation by those banks, but lending by those banks to carry speculation in derivatives, such as to hedge funds, to their own hedge funds which then loan; that after separation essentially their capital cannot be used in order to support derivatives activity. That's essentially what made it "21st Century" since there was not explicit attention to derivatives activity in the original Glass-Steagall Act. So that's all well and good.

It's was not in the House legislation, but the House legislation will do just fine without that, resting on the original Glass-Steagall; it still, by implication, is there.

Now, when somebody like Mnuchin comes up with a sophistry and says "what I was discussing with President Trump was some 21st Century version of Glass-Steagall," what he means, and I think it certainly slipped out from him in there, he means the Volcker Rule, modified in some way, loosened up in some way, and to call that "the 21st Century Glass-Steagall."

But you know, you have the testimony of one of the two drafters of the Volcker Rule, the Senator from

Oregon—Jeff Merkley—who only six months ago finally endorsed, cosponsored, the Glass-Steagall bill in the Senate, after resisting and resisting and resisting for two years, furiously, because the Volcker Rule was his baby. He finally signed and cosponsored Glass-Steagall and he made a public statement where he basically said: "We intended the Volcker Rule to replace the Glass-Steagall Act, to be the modern Glass-Steagall Act, but we are unable to determine whether it's working in that regard at all." Period. Also, Jeff Merkley and Sen. Carl Levin were the designers of the Volcker Rule. He gave up on it—it's completely unworkable. So that "21st Century Glass-Steagall" sophistry has nothing to do with Glass-Steagall.

II. Friday: Jason Ross on the LaRouche PAC Weekly Webcast

'Alexander Hamilton and the Value in Real Economic Development'

Jason Ross: When Trump was sworn in on the 20th, already a week before, Congresswoman Rosa DeLauro, a Democrat from Connecticut, had entered a bill, and there are now several proposals on the table in terms of how to finance an infrastructure build-up, a manufacturing build-up, a revitalization of the U.S. economy. There's a lot of projects that are worthwhile to be pursued; the big question is how are you going to pay for it. A trillion dollars is a lot of money; where is it going to come from? Will it come from the Treasury directly taking on that much new debt by selling Treasury bonds? What kind of interest will it have to pay on those? Is that something that's sustainable?

There are a couple of proposals being made. Rosa DeLauro, on January 13th, with 73 co-sponsors, entered a bill, HR547, for a National Infrastructure Development Bank. Her hope would be that through $50 billion in Federal bonds, and bringing in $600 billion from pension funds and other types of investors, she'd be able to capitalize a bank that could then give loans for infrastructure and purposes like that. A second proposal was made just on Tuesday, this by Senator Schumer, a Democrat from New York, with some other Democratic Senators. They made a proposal for $1 trillion; it's a proposal to make 15 million jobs. He said that he would want to put $75 billion towards schools, $200 billion towards roads, $100 billion for water treatment systems and water supply systems, $200 billion for public transit—rail and bus, $70 billion for ports and airports, $100 billion for electricity, $10 billion for VA hospitals, $20 billion for broadband, and the remaining $200 billion as a major fund for vital projects like perhaps the Gateway Project—crossing the Hudson between New Jersey and New York.

Now, how did he propose to pay for that? They said that they were going for full Federal funding. That is, not public/private partnerships, but basically through allocations. Where's that money going to come from? One idea—not that they actually said how they were going to get it—they said cutting loopholes, perhaps, to get more taxes. Now, $1 trillion is an awful lot to get from cutting loopholes. Another idea that's been promoted is the idea of cutting the corporate tax rate in order to repatriate the very large amount of profits that U.S. corporations have made overseas, that they've avoided bringing into the United States, to avoid being taxed the corporate tax rate on it. So, one idea is to drop that tax rate and offer a special incentive for companies to repatriate their profits, and then use that to finance.

These programs aren't going to work; and there's a major flaw in them that is addressed by the Hamiltonian approach. So, just going back to what Hamilton had done as Treasury Secretary, there are two aspects: One was, he made good on the public debt. He developed a way to make sure the public debt was financed, and by doing that, at the time, turned it effectively into that much circulating capital. That IOUs from the government that were trading below face value because people were unsure whether they'd ever be repaid, by developing taxes to make sure those interest payments could be made—all of those IOUs, all of that public debt, became effectively *currency*; and they could then be used in the economy for loans and that sort of purpose. Hamilton also set up a national bank that was capitalized via this public debt, and then created a currency—national bank notes for the United States—to allow loans to go out to improve the productivity of the nation. It ended up being used in his bank to finance infrastructure projects, to expand manufacturing, loans for businesses to develop and make capital investments, that sort of thing.

The projects to be financed by the bank—say, a national high-speed rail network—these are the types of

LaRouchePAC

Jason Ross

projects that are going to take years to really bring about and get operating in a full way; they're not going to make an immediate financial payback. They're not going to generate funds immediately. So, how do you finance them? The answer is in the indirect nature of its financing, via a tax that isn't on projects financed by the bank, but through a tax which secures the debt, the capital of the bank. In the long term, however, the bank will be secured through the increase in productivity which results from the investments. Take the example of the Tennessee Valley Authority. It sold bonds; it paid them back; it made good on its payments. But, more importantly, *indirectly*, the cost of the TVA was paid back through the increased productivity of the region and the entire nation, even including the increased income tax that came in from the region of the country that benefitted most from the TVA.

Let's think about what some of those projects could be. When you think about the way the human species has developed over time, the number of people that have lived on the planet has changed in dramatic ways due to very specific changes in the technologies available to us—the development of agriculture, the discoveries in health and industry, the Renaissance, the creation of science itself. These are the things that drive the human species forward. As an aspect of that, we fundamentally transform our relationship to the physical world.

So, these kinds of jumps in what we're capable of, that's the backbone of what economics is as a human science. When we think about the ways of implement-

Tennessee Valley Authority

Raccoon Mountain Pumped-Storage Plant, part of the Tennessee Valley Authority.

holes. These are the kinds of projects that mean that we are really going to develop a whole new potential as an economy.

In terms of what it means to finance these things, *the importance is in understanding what value is, and I think this is the real central key problem in economics.* Lyndon LaRouche has identified in his economic textbooks and his writings over decades, that a real definition of economic value, of the creation of wealth, comes in those activities that speed the increase of the potential population density of the human species. A physical measure of value; *not what the market thinks something is worth*, but a real metric that lies outside of what people seem to care about at the moment. This makes it into a real science.

The major aspect of that is that the value of everything in an economy lies in relation to how it is acting to bring about a future of that sort, via the capital budgeting approach made possible through a national bank of the type that we're proposing. It makes sense to think about investments paying for themselves. Some of them pay directly—a business expands and makes greater profits. But when it comes to the economic platform, the infrastructure that the country as a whole relies upon, these benefits—the benefits of science, of the space program, of going to the Moon. Going to the Moon generated incredible profits for the nation—incredible development for the nation by opening up new types of manufacturing and new technologies. But it wasn't NASA that made the money, that made a "profit"—the whole economy benefitted, and not only in a monetary type of way.

If we get away from public/private partnerships, if we get away from the idea that we're going to have some kind of deal to repatriate profits overseas—which might in part be a good idea—but the real concept behind credit, as opposed to money, is the difference

ing this in the United States, some of the projects are somewhat simple. Some might say that crossing the Bering Strait isn't the simplest of projects, but it's reasonably straightforward. This is an engineering project that we know how to build. It might present a few unique challenges given its length and given the not so hospitable climate in the area, but this is the kind of project that deserves investment—linking the world together in this way. A national high-speed rail network: If we were to build in phases, 20,000, 40,000 miles of high-speed rail, we will transform the way that we move about inside the country. We'll transform the productivity and the value of whole regions of the nation—and of the productivity and potential value of the nation as a whole.

A water management approach to the continent: Taking on the drought that's been challenging and causing quite a bit of trouble in the south, southwest and west of the United States. The ability to use desalination directly from the ocean, if needed; to get water from the Pacific and make it available. To move water along the continent as a longer-term project; to continue with studies about transforming water in the atmosphere; of inducing rainfall; of changing weather patterns. These are the kinds of broad-scale projects that aren't simply repaving a road and removing the pot-

between thinking about value lying in what it creates for the future, versus what the market thinks something is worth today.

You have to always be setting the stage for that next level to say that you're really fully developing your economy and potential.

III. Saturday: Diane Sare in Manhattan

'Destroy George Soros and the British System'

Dennis Speed: There are special actions that we're going to be taking, including at this meeting, because the nomination of Steven "Munchkin" Mnuchin to become the U.S. Treasury Secretary has been sped up. Senator Orrin Hatch says that there will be a vote on Monday; and as a result, what we've decided to do is to call an emergency mobilization, including an activists' call for the nation at 1 p.m. tomorrow.

Now, this is embedded in something a bit larger, and I'm going to reference that. Obviously, we're fighting for Glass-Steagall, but I want to talk about why that is an international battle. I want to refer to Russian Foreign Minister Sergey Lavrov and some remarks that he made before the lower house of the Russian legislature, the Duma. He said this: "We believe that as Russia, the United States, and China build their relations, this triangle should not be closed or directed towards some projects that could worry other states. They should be open and fair. I am convinced that the economic structure of Russia, the United States, and China is such that there is a great deal of complementarity in the material and economic sphere. As for international security problems, these three countries play a very important role. Russia and China have restrained attempts to introduce confrontational force-based solutions into world politics. We expect that Donald Trump, who has confirmed his commitment to focus primarily on U.S. domestic problems and to abandon interference in the affairs of other states, will do the same."

There was a response that then came from Hua Chunying, the Chinese Foreign Ministry spokesperson, and she had this to say: "China, Russia, and the United States are the leading global powers, and they are the permanent members of the UN Security Council. We

have great responsibility for global peace, stability, and development. Therefore, China intends to intensify cooperation with the United States and Russia; and to make common contribution to solving the tasks and challenges of the modern world."

That's the actual context of the meeting today; and obviously it's well known among people here, the role that Lyndon LaRouche has played for decades—nearly a half a century, actually—in creating this moment in terms of the potentials that exist in this moment.

What we're going to do is go right to Diane, our first speaker; and we're going to take up the certain context that we're actually operating in, because we intend to end the rule of the British Empire. We want people to understand what that British Empire is, and what we can do to end its rule.

Diane Sare: Thanks. I think most people in this room do not have the problem of why we're talking about the British Empire, but a lot of Americans do. For that reason, I think it's worth reflecting a little bit on the current state of affairs; what's happened with the U.S. elections, the Trump administration, and a little bit of our recent history. People may be aware that the British Prime Minister, Theresa May, has made herself the first head of state to meet with Donald Trump. What was reported is that she really wants to urge—and she said that Trump agreed with her, but I'm not sure that that's true at all—that we maintain a very strong NATO alliance. Obviously, she does not want the United States to be lifting the sanctions against Russia, or working with Russia.

She compared her hopes for her relationship with Donald Trump to be like Margaret Thatcher's relationship with the senior Bush—George H.W. Bush; where Thatcher was known for supposedly pumping iron into his spine to get him to go to war with Iraq. If people remember that first Iraq war, it came not that long after the Berlin Wall had come down. Our ambassador to Iraq, April Glaspie, gave Iraq permission to invade Kuwait. She told them, "if you were to invade Kuwait, we would not consider that a big deal; we'd consider it internal Iraqi politics and not get involved." So, Iraq invaded Kuwait. Margaret Thatcher meets with H.W. Bush, and the next thing you know we have our first Iraq war.

Then, take a leap forward to the events of 9/11. Everyone knows that Iraq had absolutely nothing to do

Diane Sare

LaRouchePAC

with that; however, they tortured some poor fellow into saying that somehow Saddam Hussein had connections to al-Qaeda. Tony Blair—again, another British Prime Minister—provided us with the so-called "evidence" of weapons of mass destruction; and another Bush, G.W. Bush, was merrily on his way to war with Iraq again. So, the British policy—from the monarchy explicitly to their so-called "elected leadership"—has had a very dubious relationship to the United States. In fact, you could say that for the last number of decades, the United States has been a pawn of a British imperial policy. One of the reasons they have been so utterly freaked out by the election of Donald Trump, is that Donald Trump is not part of the George Bush-Tony Blair-Margaret Thatcher British monarchy control so far. They don't know what he is going to do, and he's expressed explicitly an intention to work with Russia, to work with China, that he may not be willing to be a pawn of the British Empire in the same way. As Mr. LaRouche pointed out, Trump has a very big ego and probably does want to do great things. So, if he wants to do great things, he will have to do things which are a recognized benefit to the American population. I am quite certain that the policies that will benefit the American population are not the policies that will benefit what is left over from the British Empire.

My view is that it shouldn't be that difficult. What do China and Russia have to offer as a collaboration with the United States? Well, China has lifted 700 million people out of poverty in the last few decades;

Russia is actually waging a successful war against ISIS, unlike our policy of the last 15 years of supporting al-Qaeda and ISIS. China is reaching out to 100-something nations with its Belt and Road program, building very modern, advanced infrastructure. The population is optimistic; they have a future. India, which should also be included in this, is also in a similar future-oriented direction. So, that's one possible pathway for the United States to collaborate with that.

What is the shape of the so-called British Empire? Well, most of the people in the British Empire don't even want to be in it, which is what we saw with the Brexit vote and what we saw with the vote in Italy. They are bankrupt; they have—as we have in the United States—increasing problems of drug addiction, suicide, an increasing death rate. It would seem to me it's not that difficult of a choice. On the one side, you can drop dead; and on the other side, you can have a future. However, the bankrupt Wall Street lackeys of the British Empire are very desperate to cling to their sinking Titanic. Among these, one of the top collaborators or handlers of Steven Mnuchin is the British knight, George Soros. He was knighted by the Queen as early as 1965.

George Soros

As people may know, we published in a pamphlet, in 2008, an interview that Soros had done with "60 Minutes" where he talked about how he had—basically what happened is, when the Nazis invaded Hungary, his father got him a job working for one of the top Nazis. My understanding is that his first job was delivering the notices to Jewish families that it was time to get on the boxcars; and little George enjoyed doing this so much that it even unnerved his father. So, he got him a different job, which was to steal all of the paintings and jewelry and possessions of these Jewish families as they were marched off to their extermination in the camps. When the "60 Minutes" host asked him, "Did you ever need counseling? Didn't you feel horribly guilt-stricken that here you were standing, and all these people were being killed? And you were Jewish, but you were having all the people you knew being marched off to the camps?" And George said, "No, it never bothered me. If I didn't do it, someone else would have."

In his own book, he describes this time when he was 14 years old, assisting countless thousands of families off to their deaths, that this was among the happiest moments of his life. So, this is George Soros; this is who Steven Mnuchin has worked for and worked with for the last fifteen years. This explains everything about him. I know the Democrats are up in arms about what he did when he took over OneWest with the foreclosures. Well, if you think about the attitude of George Soros, stealing everyone's possessions as they're marched off to the concentration camps, that's not really that different than coming in to take over a mortgage company and watching everyone get foreclosed upon and thrown out of their homes, and not believing that there's anything wrong with it; which is the mentality of this guy who has been nominated to be Treasury Secretary.

There is an editorial—Soros has stated explicitly that he hopes the Trump administration fails. But I just wanted to give you a little sense, because LaRouche said it's the British *system* versus the American System, or versus a human system. And by British system, I don't think it's merely economic; it's philosophical, it's Bertrand Russell, who did more to destroy modern science than any other person on the planet. There's a certain approach. I just wanted to share with you, there's another essay here by George Soros, which appeared in *Business Insider*; and you get a sense of the... I mean, one, the guy is a total pathological liar. He starts the essay saying, "Well, before Donald Trump was elected President of the United States, I sent a holiday greeting to my friends that read: 'These times are not business as usual. Wishing you the best in a troubled world.' Now I feel the need to share this message with the rest of the world. But before I do, let me tell you who I am. I'm an eighty-six year-old Hungarian Jew, who became a U.S. citizen." I think he's got dual—he's got subjecthood, or whatever you call it in Britain. "I learned at an early age how important it is what kind of a political regime prevails. The formative experience of my life was the occupation of Hungary by Hitler's Germany in 1944. I probably would have perished had my father not understood the gravity of the situation. He arranged false identities for his family and for many other Jews; with his help, most survived"—except those I helped get into the concentration camps.

First of all, his relationship to this process: he is completely lying. Not that his father didn't change his identity, but that he loved working for the Nazis. Then he goes on to talk about how he escaped Hungary after it was under Communist rule—which he probably considered worse than Nazi rule—and went to the London School of Economics. Then he said, "I find the current moment in history very painful. Open societies are in crisis, and various forms of closed societies—from fascist dictatorships to mafia states—are on the rise. How could this happen?" And he talks about globalization; that people thought this would really work, but it didn't work so well, and he had been an avid supporter of the European Union from its inception. He said: "I regarded it as the embodiment of the idea of an open society, an association of democratic states willing to sacrifice part of their sovereignty for the common good. It started out at as a bold experiment in what Popper"—this was his favorite British philosopher—"called 'piecemeal social engineering.' The leaders set an attainable objective and a fixed timeline and mobilized the political will needed to meet it, knowing full well that each step would necessitate a further step forward....

"But then something went woefully wrong. After the crash of 2008, a voluntary association of equals was transformed into a relationship between creditors and debtors ..."—Oh my! Who could have ever foreseen this?

Now you have a bunch of anti-EU movements, "from the Brexit, then the Donald Trump victory"—he puts in that category—and the December 4th referendum in Italy, which people may remember. The Italian voters voted against giving up their sovereignty to the European Central Bank. So, now he says, now all these people have rejected being under a bankers' dictatorship,

"Democracy is now in crisis. Even the U.S., the world's leading democracy, elected a con artist and would-be dictator as its president. Although Trump has toned down his rhetoric since he was elected, he has changed neither his behavior nor his advisers. His Cabinet comprises incompetent extremists and retired generals.... But the U.S. will be preoccupied with internal struggles in the near future, and targeted minorities will suffer."

This is the guy who funded fifty-one of the women's groups that participated in the march on Washington last week, that had ads up on Craigslist to pay people $1,500 a week to protest at the Trump Towers and things like that. He says that Trump is going to have an affinity with dictators. "That will allow some of them to reach an accommodation with the U.S., and others to carry on without interference. Trump will prefer making deals to defending principles. Unfortunately, that will be popular with his core constituency.

"I am particularly worried about the fate of the EU, which is in danger of coming under the influence of Russian President Vladimir Putin, whose concept of government is irreconcilable with that of open society. Putin is not a passive beneficiary of recent developments; he worked hard to bring them about. He recognized his regime's weakness: It can exploit natural resources but cannot generate economic growth." Now, the standard of living in Russia has actually been improving, even though the sanctions are causing hardships. So, Putin has been doing a brilliant job, and as people know, his popularity is something like 87% or 90%. Soros asserts that Putin "felt threatened by 'color revolutions' in Georgia, Ukraine, and elsewhere. At first, he tried to control social media. Then, in a brilliant move, he exploited social-media companies' business model to spread misinformation and fake news, disorienting electorates and destabilizing democracies. That is how he helped Trump get elected."

H.G. Wells

So, this is this unbelievable, sophistical piece of garbage from George Soros, and I read it to you at that length, because what I want to discuss a little bit is what LaRouche described in a paper in last week's *EIR* magazine. It's a paper he wrote in 1997, called "The Wells of Doom." He talks about Bertrand Russell and H.G. Wells, and he's looked at some of Wells' writings in particular; and he describes Wells as not the controller of the system, he's one of its lackeys. Which is the role that Soros plays today, so Wells really enjoyed having this arrogant position. It's like being on a slave plantation, and the slave who worked the closest to the master felt it was a special privilege—even though he was still a slave—to be the one who was under the master and able to brutalize everyone else. This was the mentality of H.G. Wells. I just skimmed through yesterday, this book of his called *Anticipations*. It was written I think in 1901. He's forecasting what the state of affairs is going to be long into the future. People say he was a genius. It really makes you sick. He goes through this thing of how railroads work. He says it wasn't that mankind really needed to travel faster; there wasn't really a demand for it. But when you had the discovery of coal, you began to have a steam

engine. That was very interesting, but the coal was so heavy that you couldn't operate a steam engine on the soft roads because they would sink. So, you have to put it on rails. Since they weren't really thinking into the future, they were basing things on the horse-drawn carriage, so they set a rail gauge which was arbitrarily correspondent with a horse-drawn carriage—four feet and eight inches—which wasn't really the best idea in the world, because it made it hazardous to turn corners, and so on. But at any rate, they discovered they could build rails.

It was all just an arbitrary narrative. Then, he goes on to describe how ultimately people would figure out that you want to have independence, and you want to have highways. And you're going to have some kind of—he doesn't call it an automobile—but a vehicle; and probably people will be zooming along at seventy miles per hour. So, of course someone today could say, "Oh what a genius! He figured this out." But then in the rest of the book, he goes through all of his hypotheses about how life is going to be run, and he says this will give rise to a modern family. The father will probably have—they'll have two or three children, and as long as the wife is intelligent and mild-mannered, she'll be happy to manage the affairs of the house. It's pages and pages of this, like someone playing with Barbie dolls and describing the state of affairs. This is how the British Empire thinks.

I'll take a step back, because Wells' controller was Bertrand Russell. People have heard, we've cited these quotes from Bertrand Russell, supporting Thomas Malthus and so on: that you have to cull the herd once every generation; the state of affairs might be unpleasant, but what of it? Really high-minded people are indifferent to happiness; especially that of other people. That kind of view. The philosophy is that you can't even have language. Under Bertrand Russell, this mentality, there is no such thing as creativity—that you cannot have a new idea. That's what you get from the way Wells describes this. It isn't that someone from above said, "Hey, we should figure out how to get across the continent, connect the oceans." No! Nothing can happen which is not based on a past experience, and you can map everything according to trend lines. Which is why none of these people, for example, foresaw the disintegration of the Soviet Union and the fall of the Berlin Wall.

Think about what Lyndon LaRouche did in 1988

on Columbus Day. He's on trial in Massachusetts; they're trying to shut him down. And he's in Berlin giving a press conference saying that the Soviet economy is going to disintegrate, that the United States would help by feeding Poland in return for the reunification of Germany. At the time, I thought, "Wow! What is this? What is he doing?" This American who's running for President, standing over there in Berlin, talking about the reunification of Germany. Well, what happened a year later? The Berlin Wall is down, and a year later, Germany is reunified. And, exactly as LaRouche says, Berlin should be the capital again, Berlin becomes the capital again. What happens is, the British go on a total tear. If you remember, Maggie Thatcher and Bush, Sr., I'll never forget Bush Sr. whining with his asthmatic self, "You won't see me dancing on the Berlin Wall." They opposed the reunification of Germany, and they devised the euro system later over the dead bodies of people like Herrhausen, to make sure that you did not have a renaissance, an East-West collaboration.

It's really important, because we in this country have been very much behavior-modified by this British method of thinking. People think that nothing can happen in the future which is not based on a series of things that occurred in the past. But that's not the way history works, and it's not the way science works. This is why, for example, you cannot conduct experiments on computers, because the computer does not have anything in it that you have not programmed into it. So, a computer is not going to tell you something new. People might remember the Class A Mercedes car, where they did so-called benchmarking; they only tested the car on computers, and then they produced a whole bunch of them. But when you turned the corner, if you went over 40 miles an hour, the car would overturn—after they built them.

So, what Wells is—as Soros is today—was the enforcer, the brutalized brutalizer of the population. He says in one section of his book, "The men of the New Republic will not be squeamish either, in facing or inflicting death, because they will have a fuller sense of the possibilities of life than we possess. They will have an ideal that will make killing worth the while. Like Abraham, they will have the faith to kill, and they will have no superstitions about death. They will naturally regard the modest suicide of incurably melancholy or diseased or helpless persons as a high and courageous act of duty, rather than a crime." Then, what Mr. LaRouche quotes in this paper, "The Wells of Doom" is Wells' brilliant insight that "The new Machiavelli is all the world away from overt eroticism. The themes stress the harsh incompatibility of wide public interests with the high swift rush of imaginative passion. With considerable sympathy for the passion, I was not indulging myself in the world in artistic pornography, or making an attack on anything considered moral. I was releasing in these books a long accumulation of suppression. I was working out the collateral problems with an ingenious completeness." Glad he's so modest! "In a world where pressure on the means of subsistence was a normal condition of life, it was necessary to compensate for the removal of traditional sexual restraints. And so my advocacy of simple and easy love-making had to be supplemented by an adhesion to the propaganda of the neo-Malthusians. This I made in my anticipations that I was telling you about, and continued to write."

So, the guy is a pervert! In other words, since there's nothing beyond your existence than what is put here in front of you that's available to your senses, and none of that can be explained outside of what has come before, then there is no purpose to your life.

Now, the problem they have is that human beings actually are not computers, and human beings actually are creative, and in the United States you have had a Lyndon LaRouche who has been leading the fight for the American System for the last fifty years. So you had LaRouche's dialogue with and involvement direct in the Ronald Reagan administration, but he was working with people prior to that to create that Presidency. You had LaRouche's influence on Bill Clinton—Clinton's announcement that a new financial architecture was needed, and the attack on Clinton with Monica Lewinsky and the impeachment.

You now have a potential with the election of Donald Trump who is not a part of this British-Wall Street apparatus. There is a potential, and, I will say very emphatically, you have something going on globally which is really what's shaping the United States. What's happening here is not simply coming from the United States itself. And I think I'll leave for later a few things I want to say about the nature of man, as great poets and playwrights—people like Friedrich Schiller—understood. But I think we'll take that up later and I will stop here. *[applause]*

II. The New, Just World Economic Order

U.S.-MEXICO BORDER CRISIS

LaRouche Had It Licked in 1982!

by Gretchen Small

Jan. 31—Lyndon LaRouche burst onto the political scene in Mexico, so to speak, with a Nov. 1, 1976 prime-time address on U.S. national television on the eve of the presidential elections, in which he warned that the financier circles sponsoring Jimmy Carter's presidency were committed to plans which would lead to thermonuclear war with the Soviet Union, and death for the Third World. LaRouche cited their policies towards Mexico as exemplary of the "genocide" which these circles intended to bring about.

When President José López Portillo took office in December 1976, LaRouche found a ready Mexican partner for his proposals for reshaping U.S.-Mexican relations on a Hamiltonian basis. López Portillo was wide-open to such Mexican-U.S. collaboration, and a mutual friendship developed between these two fierce patriots of their respective nations, forged in their history-shaping, six-year battle to overcome the British monetarist global order oppressing both nations.

In López Portillo's first year in office in 1977, his government announced that Mexico had discovered huge new oil fields, and it would use that oil to carry out a 20-year crash economic development program, which would modernize Mexico's agro-industrial productive base and move it into a nuclear-powered economy.

LaRouche responded by putting forward a strategy for the United States and Mexico to negotiate an oil-

EIRNS/Ruben Cota Meza

Former Mexican President López Portillo (left) endorsed the wisdom of Lyndon LaRouche at a joint forum with Helga Zepp-LaRouche on Dec. 1, 1998 in Mexico City, Mexico.

for-technology agreement under which Mexico could exchange its oil, at fair prices, for the purchase of U.S.-made machine tools, capital goods, and equipment to modernize Mexico's agriculture. The United States could expect to export some $100 of the estimated $150 billion in such goods which Mexico would need to import over the coming decade, creating one million new high-skilled jobs inside the United States in the process, *EIR* calculated.

In LaRouche's view, the explosion of industrial production resulting on both sides of the border would not only mutually benefit these two countries. As LaRouche told a Monterrey television audience in March 1981 during one of his six trips to Mexico over the years, such an agreement could be used to set off "a change in the global strategic geometry resulting, chain-reaction

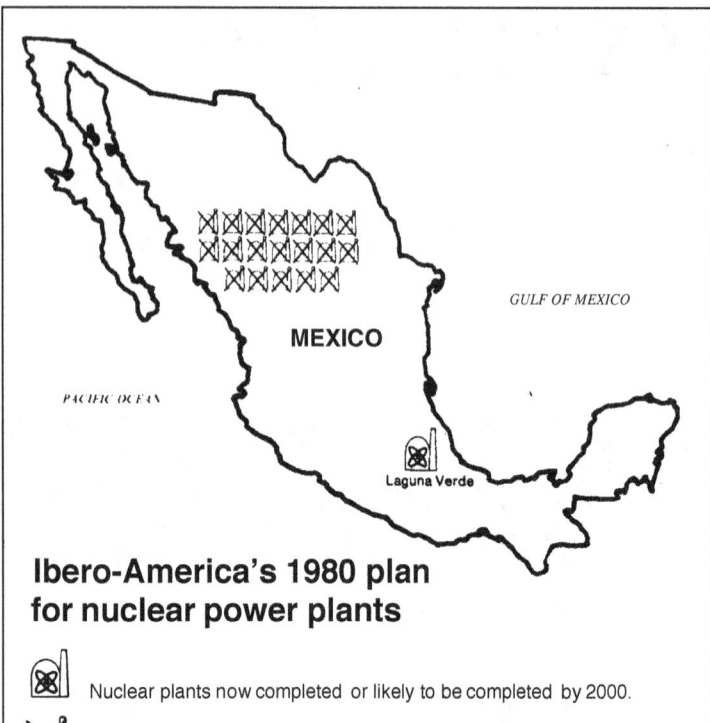

Ibero-America's 1980 plan for nuclear power plants

 Nuclear plants now completed or likely to be completed by 2000.

Nuclear plants planned, but which will not be built under present conditions.

Maps show nuclear-powered electric facilities planned by governments as of 1980 to be on-line in 2000. The symbols in the box are those not yet sited. Under fierce pressure from International bankers, these plans have been scaled down. Currently, only one plant is completed in Argentina and another in Brazil. Unless economic conditions improve, EIR estimates that Mexico, **Brazil**, and Argentina will each manage to complete their single plant in advanced stages of construction, but will be forced to abandon the rest.

EIRNS

Nuclear plants completed or planned as of 1980.

fashion, from the establishment of such a relationship."

LaRouche's audacious "oil for technology" proposal sparked excitement in sane layers on both side of the border.

Signalling whom they looked to as an ally in the United States, López Portillo's PRI party invited Lyndon LaRouche to attend the party's March 1979 congress in Mexico City. In a press conference in Mexico City, LaRouche stated that "it was important to me to take this opportunity to be in Mexico at this time, because, although the [López Portillo] government is not a power by the ordinary standard of world powers, it is at this moment, one of the most important moral forces in the world, and... one of the leading forces of the new world economic order on behalf of developing nations."

Under López Portillo's administration, from 1976

to 1982, Mexico doubled its industrial plant, created more than four million jobs, and was well on its way to full self-sufficiency in production of basic foods for its people. Plans had been drawn up to build 20 new cities, and appropriate sites were being selected, and engineers and scientists being trained, for the 20 nuclear plants planned to power the upgrading of the economic functioning of the national territory as a whole. Youth were optimistic and studying hard, as their President repeatedly told them that Mexicans "have to accustom ourselves to thinking big. We must plan large development projects with ambition and vision."

Waging Common War Against London

The Carter Administration was determined that such a threat to the British world-imperial order system would never be tolerated. In the infamous phrase of National Security Advisor Zbigniew Brzezinski, the United States could not accept "another Japan south of the border." Threats and economic warfare were not succeeding. Plans were drawn up for a finance-run "North American community" through which to grab control of Mexico's oil resources, so that no Mexican government could ever use them for development. Out of this grew the destructive NAFTA accord finally imposed against the United States, Mexico, and Canada in 1994.

President Ronald Reagan was a whole different kettle of fish, and his team was very familiar with LaRouche's U.S.-Mexico proposal. When he took office in 1981, the potential to overthrow the whole system—as LaRouche was proposing—rose to a major strategic threat to the British system. Before even being sworn in, President-elect Reagan met for three and a half hours with López Portillo; *EIR*'s sources on both sides of the border reported that the meeting was cordial and both leaders were pleased.

LaRouche visited Mexico again in 1981, this time speaking in Monterrey and Mexico City. *EIR* escalated its organizing, holding well-attended seminars in Washington, D.C. and Mexico City elaborating LaRouche's proposal, in which Mexican officials participated.

By 1982, the global financial system had reached a breakpoint, ruined, as LaRouche had warned it would be, by then-Federal Reserve chairman Paul Volcker's usurious measures. In April 1982, Great Britain

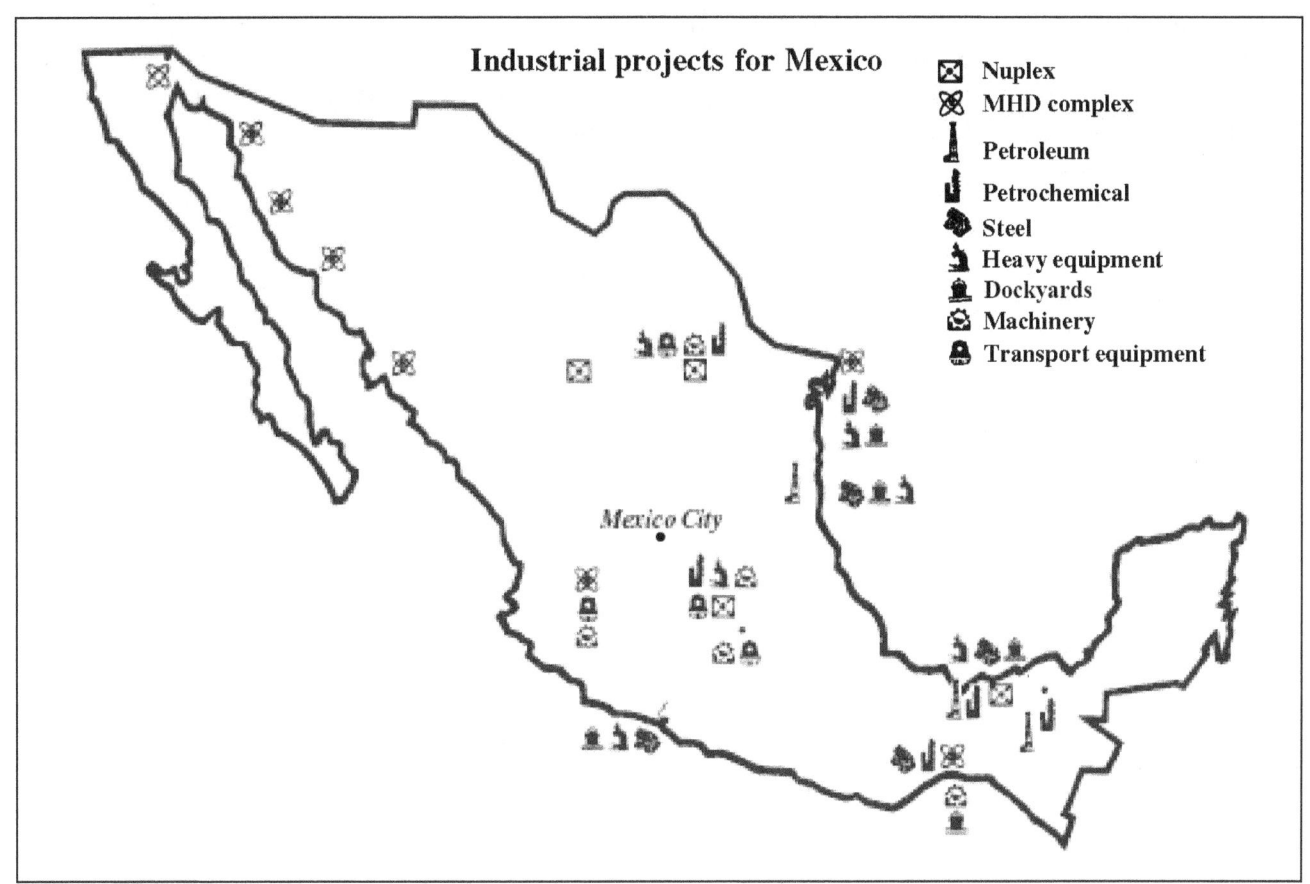

Industrial projects for Mexico

⊠ Nuplex
⊗ MHD complex
🛢 Petroleum
🛢 Petrochemical
🏭 Steel
⚙ Heavy equipment
🏛 Dockyards
⚙ Machinery
🚂 Transport equipment

Mexico City

EIRNS

1982 EIR proposal for industrial projects in Mexico, which overlapped projects proposed by President López Portillo.

launched its colonial war against Argentina, sending NATO warships steaming into the South Atlantic on the pretext of reconquering the Malvinas Islands. LaRouche immediately called for the United States to adhere to its Monroe Doctrine commitment to defend the other countries of the Americas against any oligarchic threat to their independence. LaRouche was respected as the only American leader who denounced that war for what it was, NATO's first "out-of-area" deployment to conduct "population and raw-materials wars" against developing-nation debtors in the continents of Ibero-America, Africa, and Asia. His fame soared throughout Mexico, and Central and South America.

With Ibero-America rallying around Argentina's cause, LaRouche was invited back to Mexico, this time to meet personally with President López Portillo. On May 27, 1982, in the midst of the Malvinas War, Lyndon LaRouche emerged from his 40-minute meeting with López Portillo to answer questions from 60 waiting journalists in the press room at the Mexican presiden-

tial residence, Los Pinos.

The first question asked, was what LaRouche thought about "British colonialist aggression." LaRouche denounced the war as a precedent for out-of-area NATO deployments to defend a dying financial system. He said that he and President López Portillo were on the same side, that of peace and stability, *Excélsior* reported, and that their alliance "should also embrace India, the countries of Europe, and the Non-Aligned, since only a bloc of forces of that size could succeed" against that system.

Putting *Operation Juarez* into Action

At a conference in Mexico City earlier in the week, LaRouche had proposed that the Ibero-American debtors jointly drop the "debt bomb" against London as the only means available to defeat the British NATO assault on Argentina. In his press conference at Los Pinos, he also developed the need to create "an Ibero-American Common Market which would give the countries belonging to it the possibility of defending themselves in the conflicts stemming from the international economic crisis," as *Excelsior* reported.

Lacking the courage to adopt LaRouche's strategy, Argentina capitulated to the British in early June. The war against the Mexican peso and other Ibero-American debtors escalated, exactly as LaRouche had warned it would.

LaRouche visited Mexico again in July 1982, and upon his return home, he wrote a 70-page "Mexico/Ibero-America Policy Study," famously titled *Operation Juarez*, in which he elaborated on his proposed strategy that Ibero-America join together to force through collective negotiation of debt-reorganization, and create an Ibero-American Monetary Order (including a regional bank) and common market. LaRouche chose his title "in memory of the proper alliance between the American Whigs of the United States and the Mexico liberals from whose ranks [Benito] Juarez emerged as a leading figure."

In *Operation Juarez*, LaRouche warned the United States and Ibero-America that a general, chain-reaction collapse of financial institutions was rapidly approaching. There is nothing to gain from begging from this system; if Ibero-American nations wish to survive, they must take collective action, he proposed, and impose a debt moratorium to force the great powers agreed to negotiate a new, production-based system. The policy document offered a war manual for defeating the British monetarist system, elaborating for its readers the principles of physical economics, as they are rooted in human creative mental life. Those principles are valid to this day.

On Sept. 1, 1982, López Portillo took steps to put LaRouche's *Operation Juarez* program into action, risking his life to defend Mexico from international financial speculation. In a dramatic speech to the nation, he denounced the "financial plague [which] plunders country after country" just as the rats spread the plague in the medieval era, and detailed how the country's physical economy and the population's well-being had been looted by the private banks channeling more than $54 billion to foreign financiers through capital flight. "We must organize to save our productive capacity and provide it with the financial resources to move forward," he told the nation, and then announced that as of that moment, the Wall Street-controlled Central Bank and private banking system were nationalized, and general exchange controls imposed.

López Portillo identified the unjust and obsolete financial system which sought to stop technological development, as the principal enemy of Mexico and democracy, defining democracy "as the constant economic, social and cultural betterment of the people."

From the United States, LaRouche vigorously supported López Portillo's measures as an assertion of Hamiltonian national banking and credit-policies, and detailed the measures required for a comprehensive monetary reorganization of the international system as a whole.

The NAFTA Takeover

EIR was later informed by impeccable sources, that López Portillo had called the presidents of Argentina and Brazil, and proposed that their three nations, the largest debtors in Ibero-America, jointly declare a debt moratorium, in order to force the creation of a new system, as LaRouche had recommended. Both refused, arguing in favor of staying in the system.

That October, López Portillo argued the cause of humanity's right to development in a speech before the United Nations General Assembly. "The reduction of available credit for developing countries has serious implications, not only for the countries themselves, but also for production and employment in the industrial countries." Should action to reform the system not be taken now, "it could be the beginning of a new medieval Dark Age, without the possibility of a Renaissance"; the very survival of our children, of future generations and of the human species is at stake, he warned.

Because Reagan was still president, the United States did not take immediate action against Mexico. But as soon as López Portillo was out of office in December 1982, British system forces used Henry Kissinger as their instrument to crush Mexico. López Portillo, and his measures to protect the nation, were vilified as the cause of the brutal economic crisis which then hit Mexico and worldwide, exactly as Lyndon LaRouche had warned it would hit if his proposed *Operation Juarez* debt reorganization were not carried out.

The Malthusian, free trade policies which López Portillo had fought were imposed on Mexico, and as LaRouche warned, Mexico has been destroyed. As *EIR* famously warned in its 1991 Special Report, *Auschwitz Below the Border: Free Trade Pact Is George 'Hitler' Bush's Mexican Holocaust*, NAFTA never intended to build up jobs in Mexico, but rather to destroy the productive labor force on both sides of the border, to the benefit of speculative capital. As many U.S. law enforcement officials have warned over the years, the biggest "winners" from NAFTA's free trade were the drug cartels.

By 2002, seven out of ten Mexicans had been reduced to poverty. Hunger is prevalent, and there are pockets of outright famine, because Mexico bowed to the free trade demand that it destroy its own national production, by opening the door wide to "cheaper" food imports. By 2008 (and it has worsened since), Mexico was dependent on foreign food imports to meet some 35% its overall food needs. Mexico, the original home of corn, imported 25% of its corn in 2008—and the once-corn belt states of central Mexico are the states of greatest emigration to the United States.

In discussing earlier today what U.S. policy must be, LaRouche reiterated that Mexico was destroyed by what was done to López Portillo after he left office. His policies, which were LaRouche's policies, still stand.

Despite incessant attack, to the day he died in February 2004, López Portillo never repented of his actions to defend the nation, nor of his listening to the counsel of Lyndon LaRouche. "It is now necessary for the world to listen to the wise words of Lyndon LaRouche," López Portillo told the prestigious audience attending a joint forum with Helga Zepp-LaRouche at the Mexican Society of Geography and Statistics in Mexico City on Dec. 1, 1998.

On Nov. 18, 1999, this great Mexican patriot issued an open letter to U.S. citizens, calling on them again to listen to LaRouche:

Only the transformation of the current world order into one which places the inalienable rights of people as individuals, and of nations, at the center of fundamental decisions, can initiate a new era of prosperity, peace and happiness....

In a battle for such an order, I would like to recognize the tireless and generous efforts carried out by Lyndon H. LaRouche, for whom I hope for the best as a pre-candidate for the Presidency of the United States. I wish that his voice be listened to and followed by those in the world who have the grave responsibility of stopping this situation from continuing on its calamitous course....

Kyrgyzstan and Tajikistan: The Crucial Challenge in Central Asian Development

by Ramtanu Maitra

Jan. 22—China's grand panoramic land-transport infrastructure project—a major element of the larger One Belt One Road (OBOR) vision it officially unveiled in 2013—includes developing transport arteries from China to Europe and Southwest Asia, traversing a southern route through Iran and Afghanistan.

OBOR has already linked China to Kazakhstan, Turkmenistan, and Uzbekistan—three northern and western countries of Central Asia.[1] Now, with the southern route to Afghanistan and Iran, the remaining Central Asian countries, Kyrgyzstan and Tajikistan, will also be tied into the network.

A rail link from China to Kyrgyzstan and Uzbekistan was proposed in the early 2000s. That proposal called for building a new 270 km-long rail link from Kashgar (Kashi), a business hub in China's western Xinjiang province close to the Kyrgyzstan border, to Andijan, located in the Ferghana Valley in eastern Uzbekistan, via Kyrgyzstan. The railroad will first pass through central Kyrgyzstan's Naryn, and then go south and west to Osh before entering the fertile valley and terminating in Andijan in Uzbekistan. The project remained dormant for years, perhaps because internal political instability prevented Kyrgyzstan from making such a major decision, but was revived during Kyrgyz President Almazbek Atambayev's first official visit to Beijing in June 2012. However, a

Xinhua/Li Xueren

China President Xi and Kyrgyz President Almazbek Atambayev, Jan. 6.

number of issues, including a tepid response from Kyrgyzstan's neighbor, Uzbekistan, have held back the project.

President Atambayev was in China in early January of this year and reportedly reopened discussion of the railroad. But the talks apparently have not resolved the difficult issues. According to a Jan. 20, 2017 news report by the 24.kg news agency, Kyrgyz Member of Parliament Kanybek Imanaliev, in a briefing to the Ata Meken parliamentary faction, a partner in the ruling coalition in Kyrgyzstan, said "Talks on the China-Kyrgyzstan-Uzbekistan railway came to naught."

According to the news report, Imanaliev stated, "We praise the railway project, which we like, but it's up to China to decide. It doesn't agree with the route, the gauge of the track. This question was considered in 1998 and again we have the same." Three main issues—funding, its route, and track gauge—have not been

---

1. China is also developing a substantial transport conduit from the Karakoram Highway (also known as the China-Pakistan Friendship Highway), to the Arabian Sea through Pakistan. This new rail line, called the China-Pakistan Economic Corridor (CPEC), will traverse the western side of Pakistan, running close to Afghanistan and Iran's eastern and southeastern borders.

Family of Kyrgyz nomads with its yurt—fabric over a wooden frame.

solved and are holding back the final agreement, the news item said. China prefers the 1435 millimeter track gauge, the standard gauge in China, Iran, and Afghanistan (and the most common gauge in Europe), However, all Central Asian countries have the Russian gauge, 1520 millimeters.

The railroad would be the most efficient link between China and Central Asia, because it reaches Central Asia's transport and logistics hub, Uzbekistan, the only Central Asian country that manufactures and repairs rolling stock.

The line would bring Kyrgyzstan transit fees of up to $200 million per year for the trains going through to Uzbekistan.

More important for Kyrgyzstan, the railroad would be an important link between the poorly connected North and South of the country. Such a link is particularly necessary, since the lack of adequate internal transport connections has kept Kyrgyzstan a fractious, multi-ethnic nation.

During construction, about 20,000 workers will be employed, according to at least one estimate.

Kyrgyzstan's Cultures

With a population of about six million, Kyrgyzstan is one of the three low-population nations in Central Asia, along with Turkmenistan and Tajikistan. About two-thirds of Kyrgyzstan's population is rural. The

great majority of these rural people, some of whom are also nomadic, are agricultural workers and herders, living in mountain villages in the north and east.

The origin of these settlers in this mountainous region is extremely complex. Human habitation of Kyrgyzstan stretches back into prehistory. Lake Issyk-Kul, in the northeast and not far from the Chinese border, is a cornucopia of Kyrgyzstan archaeology, and historical evidence of invaders from the past is also available in south-central Kyrgyzstan, adjoining the Ferghana Valley.

Since the 8th century A.D., many ethnic groups have either occupied or settled within Kyrgyzstan's modern borders, including Arabs, Persians of the Samanid period, and Turkic-speakers of Karakhanid Khanate. The immediate ancestors of the modern Kyrgyz people arrived in the 13th century, fleeing the invading Mongols, and this migration escalated all the way through the 16th century, this at a time when trade from the Silk Road began to enter Kyrgyz territory from the west.

Even today, Kyrgyzstan's population is not truly integrated. Ninety-five percent of the country's surface is at least 1,000 meters (3,280 feet) above sea level. There are a few isolated lowlands along Kyrgyzstan's western and northern borders. In the southwest is the fertile Ferghana Valley, which Kyrgyzstan shares with Uzbekistan and Tajikistan. The site of extensive pastures and numerous farms and towns, the Ferghana Valley receives most of its water from streams that flow into it from the surrounding mountains. Along Kyrgyzstan's frontier with Kazakhstan are the valleys of the Chu and

Shopping in the Sino Ocean bazaar in Bishkek, capital of Kyrgzystan.

Talas rivers. The valleys are densely populated and include many farms, villages, and small cities.

Of the non-Kyrgyz nationalities found in Kyrgyzstan, the largest ethnic groups are Uzbek (14.4% of the country's population) and Russians (6.4%). Ethnic Russians first came to the Central Asian region as representatives of the Russian Empire, with the aim of overseeing colonization. Few actually settled there, other than in a military capacity for the Empire. With the founding of the Soviet Union, millions of Russians were settled throughout Central Asia in accordance with Moscow's Sovietization policy. In Kyrgyzstan, they settled mainly in the North, in Bishkek the capital, and in the Chu and Ferghana valleys.

CNTV

Roadbuilding, financed by China, to integrate Kyrgyzstan.

Connecting Kyrgyzstan with Roads

This diversity among Kyrgyz nationals—stemming largely from a lack of physical integration of the population, and abetted by difficult terrain and the continuing existence of a nomadic agricultural and herding sector—makes development in Kyrgyzstan a difficult challenge. To create an environment for effective investment, China has concentrated on developing new roads to integrate Kyrgyzstan both internally and with its neighbors. In June 2015, China announced that it would provide nearly $300 million in credit to help Kyrgyzstan build a strategic north-south road for trade between the two major cities, Bishkek and Osh, which will connect with Kyrgyz roads into Kazakhstan and Tajikistan. This road is now being built.

China also helped to construct two other roads within Kyrgyzstan—Osh-Sarytash-Irkeshtam and Bishkek-Naryn-Torugart. These were funded in part by China and were built by a workforce of thirty percent local workers and seventy percent Chinese workers, with sixty percent of raw materials imported.

Beyond these modest developments, however, Kyrgyzstan has yet to benefit in a major way from the China OBOR policy. There are many problems. About forty percent of Kyrgyzstan's GDP comes from expatriates sending money home, and the overall poverty of the nation, combined with the associated lack of modern skills, is a serious hindrance to economic development.

Reviving Industrial Production

Kyrgyzstan is a victim of both the collapse of the Soviet Union and its own lack of skilled-manpower. There is a great deal of idle manufacturing capacity, particularly in the antimony and silicon processing plants, various medium-sized factories, and cotton and textile production lines in the South. According to one news report, when Chinese Foreign Minister Wang Yi visited Kyrgyzstan in May 2015, Kyrgyz economic officials suggested that Beijing relocate forty or so manufacturing operations from China to Kyrgyzstan. Kyrgyz Economy Ministry officials evaluated the proposal as a win-win project, reasoning that China would gain an important manufacturing base in Kyrgyzstan, while the Central Asian nation would benefit from the revival of idle industrial capacity.

Resistance in Kyrgyzstan

There are efforts to sabotage Kyrgyz-Chinese relations, as indicated by a May 2012 *Asia Times* article titled "Anti-China mood threatens push for Kyrgyz railway link" that was reprinted by Kyrgyz news agency Kabar It said, "Anti-Chinese fever has been on the rise again and, according to Kyrgyz observers, threatens to be a barrier to the single-most important infrastructure project between the two countries—the China-Kyrgyz-

Central Asia and the Caucasus

gyzstan and has begun to crack down on Chinese firms doing business in Kyrgyzstan. Several firms found themselves in hot water for not hiring enough locals. In January 2014, Zhongda, the Chinese-owned oil company, opened an oil refinery in Kara Balta. It faced immediate protests over pollution and for not giving Kyrgyz nationals enough opportunities. Circumstances surrounding the protests were suspicious, but whatever the reason for the protests, the company responded to employment complaints. In 2013, as the project was nearing completion, the workforce consisted of 30% locals and 70% Chinese. By 2015, the 700 employees were split 70-30 in favor of locals.

stan-Uzbekistan railway line, which will pave the way for radical geopolitical changes in Central Asia, with ripple effects further afield."

One controversy that surrounds the China-Kyrgyzstan-Uzbekistan rail project is the fear among some Kyrgyz that their government has agreed to hand over at least three separate large gold, aluminum and iron deposits to Chinese companies in exchange for construction of the railway. Gold production provides forty percent of the nation's export earnings and represents twenty percent of its GDP. An effort to whip up fear within the Kyrgyz population that China is only interested in the region's natural resources, including the gold fields, has already had some effect. Aware of public perception on this issue, China has sought to address it.

The same *Asia Times* article also stated, "Kyrgyzstan has seen the influx of tens of thousands Chinese traders, while every major Chinese investment project in the country—be it building a road, a factory or laying electricity transmission lines—invariably brings in thousands more. At least around 90,000 Chinese nationals are staying illegally in Kyrgyzstan, according to the Kyrgyz Ministry of Justice. The influx makes migration a dangerous issue, exacerbated by the fact that hundred thousands of Kyrgyz people have to migrate to Russia and Kazakhstan in search of jobs."

China is aware of this anti-China mood within Kyr-

China Learns to Communicate

China is also making other efforts to overcome hostility within Kyrgyzstan. In parallel with the infrastructure development and trade initiatives, China has established two Confucius Institutes in Bishkek, the capital—at the Bishkek Humanities University and Kyrgyz National University—with subsidiary branches in Osh and Jalal-Abad. Part of the international network of Confucius Institutes, they are focused on teaching the Chinese language to young Kyrgyz, using Kyrgyz-Chinese textbooks and leveraging faculty and administrators brought in on two-year cycles from the partner institutions, Xinjiang University and Xinjiang Normal University.

The number of Chinese-speaking Kyrgyz has remained tiny, compared to the number of Kyrgyz who can speak Russian and English, but it is growing, reflecting the opportunities that young Kyrgyz see in China or with Chinese firms in Kyrgyzstan. While the Confucius Institutes focus on language learning to prepare students to use Chinese in a business setting, teachers also stimulate interest in other aspects of China's culture and history.

Mountainous Tajikistan's Glorious Past

The eight million people of Tajikistan, Kyrgyzstan's neighbor to the south, are vastly different from the people of other Central Asian nations, although many

CC/Hardscarf

Issyk-Kul in Tien Shan mountains, a cornucopia of Kyrgyz archaeology.

oldest city of Tajikistan (more than 5,500 years old), is located in the valley of the Zeravshan River (near Samarkand). Penjikent was the last city on the way from Samarkand to the mountains of Kohistan.

Called the jewel of Tajikistan, the ancient city of Ura-Tyube (now Istaravshan), is located in the north of Tajikistan, in the foothills of the Turkestan Ridge. The city celebrated its 2,500th birthday in 2001. It was founded in the 6th century B.C. by Cyrus the Great, the Achaemenid king of Persia, when it was known as Cyropolis, or equivalently Kurushkada. When Alexander the Great conquered Central Asia in the late 4th century B.C., Kurushkada was already a big, well-fortified city.

In the days of Arabian sovereignty, Ura-Tyube became a province of the Arabian caliphate. At that time, Islamic architecture began to appear—mosques, madrassas, mausoleums, and minarets. The city's most rapid development took place under the rule of the first Tajik Samanid dynasty (9th-10th centuries). But in the 13th century the city was destroyed by the armies of Chingghis Khan. Ura-Tyube rose from the ashes in the 14th-15th centuries with the coming of powerful Timurid Empire.

Near Ura-Tyube is the city of Khujand (Leninabad in the Soviet period). Its position at the crossroads of well-known trade routes between the East and the West made Khujand one of the major economic and cultural centers of Central Asia and a major center on the Silk Road. The silk products and jewelry made by the craftsmen of Khujand were known not only in the East, but thoughout the world. The names of the city districts speak of the former significance of those crafts—Zargaron (jewelers), Pilakashon (silk-winders), and Sangburon (masons). Khujand was founded more than 2,500 years ago. It was there when the army of Alexander the Great arrived on the banks of the Syr Darya.

The northern segment of the old Silk Road is known today as the Pamir Highway. It runs 1,250 km from Tajikistan's capital, Dushanbe, to Osh in the south of Kyrgyzstan. Today, the Pamir Highway fa-

Tajiks can be found in Kyrgyzstan and Uzbekistan. The Tajiki language is of Indo-Iranian rather than Turkic origin, and is close to the Farsi spoken in Iran and the Dari spoken in Kabul. According to Tajik historians, "the formation of the Tajik nation was completed during the rule of the Samanids"—that is, the Samanid dynasty, founded by Ismail Samani in Bukhara of the 9-10th centuries—and are the heirs of its culture and its lofty poets, such as Rudaki and Ferdowsi, who are also loved in Iran today. The Samanid dynasty became the capital of all Central Asia, including Khurasan, the Ferghana Valley, Khwarazm, and most of what is now Afghanistan. Highly literate and given to careful record-keeping, the Samanid bureaucrats took as their symbol the ink bottle.

During the great era of Silk Road trade, parts of Tajikistan lay on its historic route, linking Bactria, Tokharistan, Soghd, Istaravshan, and Ferghana with India, Afghanistan, and China. The Soghd route went from Samarkand to Kokand through Penjikent and further on the road leading to the Ferghana valley through Varz, Ura-Tyube, Khujand, Konibodom, and Isfara. The other route connected Termez and Kashgar (China) through Hissar and Dushanbe (the capital of Tajikistan today).

Tajik cities on the Silk Road are precious pearls framed by picturesque landscapes. Among them are Penjikent, Ura-Tyube, and Khujand. Penjikent, the

Laying the Central Asia-China Gas Pipeline's Line D across Tajikistan.

half of China's natural gas imports come through this expanding array of pipelines, thousands of kilometers in length, that spans Turkmenistan, Uzbekistan, and Kazakhstan.

With Lines A, B, and C in operation, the new 1,000 km Line D will carry gas from Turkmenistan's Galkynysh gas field to China through southern Uzbekistan, northern Tajikistan, and eastern Kyrgyzstan. It will be capable of transporting 30 billion cubic meters, and when completed, this will raise CACGP's gas exports to China to a total of 85 billion cubic meters per year.

cilitates the transit of consumer goods from China to Central Asian markets. In certain sections, particularly where it crosses international frontiers, the road is of good quality. But much of the highway is unpaved, and it takes several days to journey from Dushanbe to Kashgar, the westernmost urban center in China. The distance is not so great, around four hundred miles, but the altitude and poor road quality makes for slow traveling.

Natural Gas Line D Crosses Tajikistan

Tajikistan's gas and oil resources were never developed by the Soviet Union, and as a result, the vast bulk of the country's reserves, mostly buried in the Amu Darya basin in the southwest of the country, have remained unexplored. Nonetheless, Tajikistan has remained important in China's energy plans. The construction of a new $3.2 billion Chinese gas pipeline through Tajikistan is the most significant Chinese investment in the country so far. This pipeline is the fourth ("D") section of the Central Asia-China Gas Pipeline (CACGP) that began operation in late 2009. Today, more than

The mountainous terrain of Tajikistan, however, where the longest section of Line D (410 kilometers) is being built, presents an expensive and difficult undertaking for project planners and engineers. It will not simply mean installing pipeline along relatively flat steppe and desert, as was the case with early phases of CACGP, but will instead necessitate costly and sophisticated engineering. These challenges include "the creation of 47 tunnels with a total length of 76 kilometers. In 24 of these cases, the tunnels will be underwater," as Tajik President Emomali Rahmon himself emphasized at the ground-breaking ceremony on

Central Asia-China Gas Pipeline

September 13, 2014, in company with Chinese President Xi Jinping. Tajikistan will not receive any of the gas, but will earn transit revenues.

Tajikistan Orients Toward China

Beyond securing a steady stream of transit revenue from Line D of the CACGP, Tajikistan is also seeking hydro-power development to generate electricity for itself and for export. Tajikistan gets a significant amount of annual rainfall and that drains into the Amu Darya, a 2,400 kilometer river, with many significant tributaries, which flow westward from Tajikistan through Uzbekistan to the Aral Sea. But the heavy withdrawal of water by Uzbekistan leaves virtually nothing to reach the Aral Sea, which has shrunk by almost 70 percent over recent decades.

Xinhua

Tajikistan President Emomali Rahmon and China President Xi Jinping at Phase 1 completion ceremony of Dushanbe power plant built by TBEA.

Because Tajikistan is short of electricity, a major dam is needed on the Vakhsh (Surkhob) River, a major tributary of Amu Darya. This new dam, the Rogun Dam, will generate 3,600 MW of electric power. Construction began on Rogun in 1980, but stalled at the end of the Soviet era. Uzbekistan opposes construction of the dam since it fears the filling of the reservoir every summer, when rainwater is available on the upstream side, will jeopardize Uzbekistan's water requirements.

Rogun Dam is one of about 10 hydro projects, either operating or planned, in the Vakhsh River Cascade. Vakhsh River hydro projects include operating projects (600 MW Baipaza, 240 MW Golovnaya, 24 MW Perepednaya, 15 MW Centralnaya, 3,000 MW Nurek); projects under construction (3,600 MW Rogun, 670 MW Sangtuda 1, 220 MW Sangtuda 2); and proposed projects (200 MW Nurobad 2, 850 MW Shurob).

The Rogun project includes the embankment dam, hydraulic tunnels of 1,100 to 1,500 meters, an underground powerhouse with six units, and other plant and auxiliary equipment. A consortium of Tractebel Engineering France (Coyne et Bellier) and ELC Electroconsult Italy is providing technical assistance to project developer OJSC Rogun HPP.

China is not participating in the construction of the dam itself, but has made a major contribution to the project by financing power lines from Sangtuda 1 and 2 hydroelectric power plants on the Vakhsh River in the Danghara district. China's Exim Bank financed—and

Chinese electric company Tebian Electric Apparatus (TBEA) built—the power transmission line between Tursunzada and Khudjand at a cost around $270 million. Another transmission line, Sangtuda-Khatlon-Lolazor, was also financed and built by Chinese companies and became operational in June 2008. The two lines have allowed energy flow from southern Tajikistan to northern areas of the country, thus eliminating, or at least decreasing, Tajikistan's dependence on Uzbekistan's supplies.

Yet another power transmission line that runs between Khudjand and Ayuni, also financed and built by the Chinese, was completed in 2011, offering an alternative route for electricity transmission from energy-abundant southern Tajikistan to the energy-deficient north. In addition, TBEA has built two coal-fired thermal power stations in Dushanbe to provide power to the capital, one of which began operating in 2014 and the other in December 2016, together producing about 400 MW of electric power.

China-Tajikistan economic relations have now gone beyond cooperation in Tajikistan's energy sector. The Tajik government announced earlier in 2016 that China plans to invest $500 million to build seven industrial concerns in the north of the country. Last June, construction began on a metals processing plant in the northern town of Istiqlol, which is being completed with $200 million dollars from China. Tatyana Panteleyeva, head of the economic development department in the Istiqlol city administration, said that this

NWPower/www.ompower.cc/english

Tajik and Chinese at work at coal-fired power plant in Dushanbe, Tajikistan.

The Uyghur secessionists, seeking to break Xinjiang Province off from China, have now joined hands with these foreign-funded and foreign-promoted terrorists. Uyghur militants were suspected of involvement in a terrorist attack on the Chinese embassy in Bishkek, the Kyrgyz capital, on August 30, 2016.

Meanwhile, the opium explosion in Afghanistan, under the watch of NATO and the United States since 2005, has not only created a brigade of armed smugglers who often work in collusion with the terrorists to protect each other, but has corrupted a vast section of the security apparatus and bureaucracy in Central Asia. The deluge of drug-generated cash has also strengthened the Islamist extremists. The Pamir Highway, sometimes called the "heroin highway," winding its way up through very high altitude terrain, is used to bring Afghan heroin to Osh in Kyrgyzstan on edge of the Ferghana Valley. Osh has been recently dubbed the "drug capital of Central Asia." It is anybody's guess who is on the take in allowing the drug traffic.

was only the start. "Here, across 70 hectares of land, there are plans to create a Tajik-Chinese industrial zone. We will build five industrial enterprises," Panteleyeva was quoted as saying by RFE/RL's Tajik service, Ozodi. Clearly, Tajikistan is veering increasingly toward China for building its economic strength.

The Security Threats

Both Tajikistan and Kyrgyzstan have been suffering security threats for years now. The five-year civil war in Tajikistan (1991-96) not only devastated the country economically and politically, it created a continuing security vacuum. There are two major security concerns. In the Ferghana Valley, where Kyrgyzstan, Uzbekistan, and Tajikistan meet, extremist varieties of the Islamist movement have emerged. Islamist extremist groups, preaching the heresy of Wahhabism and seeking to create a Caliphate based on Wahhabism, have been funded by Saudi Arabia and some other Gulf countries. British intelligence-controlled Hizb ut-Tahrir, preaching the same violent form of Islamism, is active throughout the region. These extremists have been indoctrinated, and are financed to buy weapons and explosives, and to obtain military training in the ungoverned areas of Afghanistan and Pakistan.

Russia, badly affected by the flood of heroin northward into its territory, has long placed troops along Tajikistan's 1,344 km border with Afghanistan. Seven thousand Russian troops patrol the border and Moscow has announced that the number will go up to 9,000 by 2020. The Collective Security Treaty Organization (CSTO), which currently has six member-states—Armenia, Belarus, Kazakhstan, Kyrgyzstan and Russia—has held several exercises aimed at facing off a veritable drug invasion from the south. Despite this, heroin continues to flow into Central Asia, Russia, and beyond into Europe.

To provide security to the Eurasian landmass, the Shanghai Cooperation Organization (SCO) was founded in 2001 by China, Russia, and all the Central Asian states except Turkmenistan. The SCO forum demands cooperation on counter-terrorism policy and holding joint military exercises.

III. Italy and the Death Crisis of the Euro

European Populations Hope for U.S. Help to End Euro Tyranny

by Claudio Celani

Jan. 29—As Italian Member of the European Parliament, Marco Zanni, told *EIR* in an exclusive interview (see below), the populations of Europe are looking with hope to the new U.S. Administration, as a potential ally in their fight for freedom from the tyrannical Euro system.

As Mr. Zanni explains, the Euro is going to be finished, at the latest, after this year's round of general elections in key European countries—such as France, Germany, and possibly Italy—which might bring an anti-Euro majority to the European Council. However, the Euro might implode even before that—for instance, if the European Central Bank (ECB) is forced to suspend its Quantitative Easing (QE) policy, or the so-called "Italian banking crisis" gets out of control, or a major zombie bank goes bust—or a combination of all three.

Although the ECB confirmed its monetary expansion policy at its last board meeting in January, growing inflation figures might make it impossible for ECB chairman Mario Draghi to continue keeping zombie banks afloat, and might force him to "taper" away from zero interest rates and "Quantitative Easing" (QE) asset purchases on the open market. Pressure is increasing from Germany for the ECB to stop its QE program if inflation rises close to the 2% "target."

Not only has Draghi's zero interest-rate policy almost destroyed traditional banking in Germany—forcing depositors to choose between losing money or investing in high-risk assets—but half of the one trillion euro of the ECB Assets Purchase Program (APP) has gone to support the City of London, as Draghi himself revealed in his letter to Zanni and Vanni (see interview).

The APP works in such a way that the ECB purchases a quota of sovereign, corporate, and asset-backed securities from banks, in order to provide those banks with liquidity. The ECB does not purchase the bonds directly, but does it through respective national central banks ("The Eurosystem"). Banks are immediately provided with liquidity by the ECB, and balances among national central banks (NCBs) are settled through the so-called "TARGET2" clearing system.

Draghi reported that "almost 80% of [the] bonds [were] purchased by national central banks, and roughly half of the purchases were from counterparties located outside the euro area, most of which mainly access the TARGET2 payments system via the Deutsche Bundesbank."

For further explanation, Draghi refers in his letter to a March 2016 ECB monthly report, which says: "Credit institutions domiciled out-

CC/Eric Chan

European Central Bank in Frankfurt, Germany.

side the euro area participate in TARGET2 via a Eurosystem NCB [national central bank], not least in the case of major international banks operating in the City of London."

So far, the ECB has provided European banks with 1.4 trillion of liquidity through the APP. The program will continue at least throughout 2017, so that at the end of the year the banks will have received almost 2 trillion, which means that the City of London has received almost 1 trillion from the ECB!

At the same time, the ECB, the EU Commission and the German government have entered into a confrontation with Italy on the issue of the Italian banking crisis and on austerity. The Italian government is refusing to apply EU rules to "bail in" (confiscate) depositors and bondholders, and has demanded more budget flexibility in order to face two emergencies: refugees, and earthquake aid and reconstruction.

The ECB, the EU Commission, and the German government insist on implementing EU bail-in and budget rules.

Creative Commons
Earthquake in central Italy in August 2016.

This became grotesque when, in the middle of earlier earthquake and bad weather damage in central Italy in mid-January, the EU Commission rejected the Italian budget plan and demanded a "correction" of 3.4 billion euro.

It has become more than evident that a continued membership in the Euro system is an obstacle to the life of the Italian population and to Italy's survival as a functioning nation.

Italian Catastrophe

A poll published by *Eurispes* Jan. 27, says that the incomes of 43% of Italians don't last to the end of the month. EU-imposed austerity has forced Italian families to reduce consumption, which the report highlights as follows: 38% have reduced their medical expenses; 70.9% meals at restaurants; 68.6% travel and holidays; and 62% hairdressers. One of every ten young persons or couples cannot afford to rent housing, and go back to live with their parents or their in-laws.

Italy's budget constraints under EU law make it im-

possible to reverse an economic stagnation that became a depression after 2011, and is now making it impossible even to deal with the earthquake emergency.

Since August 2016, the earthquakes have never stopped in central Italy. The last shocks occurred Jan. 18—four shocks of over 5.0 within two hours. This latest quake occurred in the midst of a snowstorm which had hit central and southern Italy, creating serious problems both for the quake-affected population and for the nation in general. One of the shocks unleashed a major avalanche which struck a hotel under Mount Gran Sasso (2,914 m), killing twenty-nine.

The the snowstorm collapsed electrical lines in the Abruzzo region, initially leaving 300,000 persons without power. Electricity has since been slowly restored, but not to all villages. The snowstorm has isolated many villages in the Apennines, and is especially endangering cattle herds in the earthquake areas, threatened both by the cold and the lack of water.

In this situation, the EU insistence that Italy cut its budget further—when it should instead increase it in order to face the new emergencies—has been extremely provocative, and is feeding the already-overwhelming anti-EU sentiment. Exemplary was the Jan. 18 op-ed by Antonio Cangini, editor of *La Nazione* and *Il Resto del Carlino*, a national daily read especially in central Italy. Cangini wrote that the post-Glass-Steagall era is over, but the EU has failed to recognize it—and should be buried.

With Brexit and the election of Donald Trump in the U.S.A., "a global historic phase is being closed." Cangini continued:

A chaotic as well as dramatic phase, which has brought us two poisoned fruits: the economic crisis and the European crisis. For the former, we must thank the United States. In order to avoid a repetition of the 1929 crisis, President Roosevelt had the sacred Glass-Steagall Act enacted in 1933, separating investment banks from commercial banks. Bill Clinton repealed it in 1999, opening the way to globalization, and, less than a decade later, to the implosion of the U.S. financial system, full of toxic and non-performing assets....

To save the banks, attention was shifted to the sovereign debt of states, beginning the suffering of southern and Catholic European countries. No systemic correction has been implemented since, just palliative measures such as the Dodd-Frank bill in 2010. Whatever judgment one may have on Trump's victory, it represents a shift, a radical correction of route. Instead, no shift is on the horizon in old Europe, where the route is still the same.

The EU is dead and its "corpse is beginning to stink—and holding its funeral might be the only way to start life again. The only problem: there is no gravedigger around to do it," Cangini wrote.

Cangini correctly focusses on the repeal of Glass-Steagall in the U.S.A., but he forgets that the repeal of similar banking separation systems in Italy, and in all European countries, was imposed by EU Treaties.

A Bank of Italy official did recall this, however, in a hearing before the joint Finance Committee of the Italian Chamber and the Senate, on Jan. 17. Answering a question from Deputy Alessio Villarosa (M5S), on whether the old bank-separation system would have prevented the current Italian banking crisis, the Bank of Italy's head of supervision, Carmelo Barbagallo, answered that the old system of bank separation was ended by EU guidelines—but he let it be understood that he favors the old system. "What Deputy Villarosa said on the 1936 Banking Act is very interesting," Barbagallo said. The old system "was changed in order to implement a European guideline. Separation between banks and industries, long- and short-term [credit], and banks of public interest are not European concepts. Already in the mid-'80s they were not European concepts. If Italy is a member of the EU... one can have a different personal view, but this is a fact."

So re-introducing a Glass-Steagall-like system separating commercial banks from speculative banks, is incompatible with membership in the Euro. Even defensive measures such as the Italian government decision to protect bondholders in the bail-out of Monte dei Paschi di Siena bank, which goes against EU rules, and to allocate a 20 billion fund to prevent insolvency, won't work.

Worse, they are seen by the population as a favor to bankers. The most widespread slogan at a demonstration of earthquake victims Jan. 25, in front of the national Parliament, was: "The government finds 20 billions for the banks, but not for us!" Indeed, not only is emergency housing not going up on schedule, but very little has been done to protect the cattle which are now dying in the cold wave.

Many in Italy compare the current failures with the approach adopted after the L'Aquila earthquake of 2009, when 5,600 quake-proof apartments were built in 100 days, and families were able to move in before winter struck. This was done through a military-style mobilization under a centralized Civil Protection Department (CDD) with emergency powers.

The difference between then and now is called former Prime Minister Mario Monti. Monti, the EU butcher, cut the budget of the CDD and deprived it of powers in 2011-12. Now, the CDD head no longer has sufficient emergency powers to bypass bureaucracy and get done what's necessary in a short time.

The social and political climate is explosive and will become more so as long as Italy stays in the Euro, a climate ready to fill the sails of the anti-Euro parties in the next general elections, which might come as early as next summer.

Italy Must Leave the Euro and Enact Glass-Steagall

Paul Gallagher interviewed Member of the European Parliament Marco Zanni on Jan. 26. The interview *has been edited.*

Paul Gallagher: Hello, this is Paul Gallagher of *Executive Intelligence Review*, and this is LaRouche PAC Television. We have with us this morning from Brussels, an Italian Member of the European Parliament (MEP), Marco Zanni, who for the past number of years has represented a political movement, a political party in the Italy which has generally thought that Italy should exit from the Eurozone,

EIRNS/Julienne Lemaître

Italian Member of the European Parliament Marco Zanni.

the European common currency, in order to develop its own economy, and also has proposed that Italy adopt a Glass-Steagall regulation and regulate its banking system in that way. He has recently taken principled opposition to some of the things which that movement has done, but these are his principles. And we are going to talk this morning about the state of the fight for those principles in Italy, and in Europe as a whole.

Marco Zanni, thank you for speaking with us this morning.

MEP Marco Zanni: Good morning everybody, and thank you very much for the opportunity to address U.S. citizens and the U.S. people about what is happening in Italy right now, and also what is happening in the European Union (EU), in the Eurozone. Because I think that 2017 for Europe will be a very important and challenging year.

We will have general elections in a lot of important country-members of the European Union. We will start in March with general elections in the Netherlands, then we will have France, then maybe at the end of

June, early general elections in Italy, after the ruling presented yesterday by the Italian Constitutional Court. Now we have a constitutional electoral law ready to be used, so probably President Mattarella will call for early elections in June, and then we will have elections in Germany in September. And there is a huge possibility that some of the so-called "euroskeptical" parties will gain power in one of these countries. So it will be very important.

In the mean time, I think that the economic and the macroeconomic situation in the European Union, and especially in the periphery of the European Union, will deteriorate, again. So the situation will be very, very dangerous. And the support for the so-called euro-skeptical parties in this situation could be even stronger in the picture. So it will be a very important year, a very challenging year, and let's hope that people will vote during this stream of general elections, in order to change what we would like to see changed in the policies addressed by these new parties that are rising in the political scenario of the European Union.

The first thing is getting rid of the Eurozone, getting rid of the euro. The euro is collapsing; the euro makes no economic sense. There are a lot of papers, important papers starting with James Meade's research in 1957, more than 60 years ago, that show us that the European Economic and Monetary Union is not sustainable, because we are not a United States. We are not a sort of federal state, we do not have instruments in place that could make this common currency work, and this common currency only gives advantages to Germany and to core Europe, while depressing and constraining people in countries of peripheral Europe. So the euro is not sustainable. We want to get rid of the euro.

And the other important point is the banking system. As you may know—in the United States *Monte dei Paschi* is also a well-known name—we have a very dangerous problem in the European Union and in Italy: Our banking system is collapsing and is clearly in a sort of state of default. We have a huge quantity of so-called non-performing loans, and we have a banking system that is not focussed on the real economy, as it should be, but is instead focussed on derivatives, on speculation, and on a sort of financialization of the economy.

youtube

Clashes erupted between police and protesters who rallied against Italian Prime Minister Matteo Renzi's visit to the northern Italian city of Bergamo near Milan, May 2016, as he launched his party's campaign for the Constitutional Referendum. Several protesters were injured, according to local media.

And that is really wrong. And the effects of such a financial and banking system are damaging the European people, the Italian people, and the European project. So, we need to act.

Gallagher: Marco, can I ask you, in Italy itself, the party that in recent years you've been an activist in, the Five Star Movement in Italy, has generally called for Glass-Steagall reorganization, called for leaving the euro, and in a short time it has gotten to be arguably the largest vote-getting party in Italy. Do the Italian people at this point want out of the euro? What is the state of the organizing there?

Zanni: Looking at the last polls by Euromonitor—that is a private company monitoring support for the European Union and the Eurozone in the European countries—so the last poll that was published at the end of October 2016, showed that the support for Italy exiting the Eurozone is rising. We are close to 50% of the Italian citizens who want to exit from the euro, and 50% that want to stay, or that think that the euro is something good or that it is helping Italy and Italian people to stay alive.

Let me say that just one year ago, these polls showed that the support for the Eurozone was close to 70%. So there has been a strong drop in the support for the Eurozone in Italy. I think that looking at what is happening in Italy, and looking at the political support that Italian euro-skeptical parties are gaining—now the majority of Italian citizens want to exit the euro, to end this really disastrous experience that we have had for more than 70 years.

So I think that, looking at the possibility in the next general election, there could be a majority in the Italian Parliament that will support Italy's exiting the Eurozone. So there is a strong possibility that before the end of 2017, Italy will leave the euro.

Gallagher: We've heard a couple of statements recently, both from new President Trump in the United States and also from the person he nominated, or is expected to nominate to be Ambassador to the EU—both of them talking about that breakup and countries leaving—that that is what they expect. But you and a colleague just received a letter from the President of the European Central Bank, Mario Draghi, which seemed apparently to be a kind of a threat to prevent Italy from getting out of the Eurozone. Could you tell us what the situation with that is?

The ECB Threatens Italy

Zanni: It was to a written question that I sent to Mr. Mario Draghi, the president of the European Central Bank (ECB), at the end of November 2016, and the first important thing in the reply of Mr. Draghi, is that he stated clearly, publicly, that the euro is *not* irreversible. Usually the President of the ECB, the President of the European Commission Mr. Juncker, and all the EU used to say that the euro is irreversible, so no one can withdraw from the single currency. In this letter, in his reply, Mario Draghi is basically saying that the euro is reversible, so that a sovereign country that democratically decides to leave the euro can do it—so it's feasible. That's the first important thing that emerged from the reply of Mr. Draghi.

The second point regards the TARGET2 balances. TARGET2 balances, in my view, are not debts or credits, that Italian people or Italian small and medium-size enterprises (SMEs) have with regard to German creditors or German citizens or German SMEs; but they're just an accounting flow, an accounting record of debts and credits already settled.

So Mario Draghi knows very well that what he stated about TARGET2 balances is not true, but he cannot say anything different, because if he is going to say that TARGET2 balances are not debts or credits, or are not payable, then the system will collapse immediately.

There is a statement by a very important German economist, Mr. Hans-Werner Sinn, who is one of the five economic advisors of Mrs. Merkel, and basically, a couple of months ago during a conference, he was asked about the huge amount of TARGET2 credits that Germany has with regard to the other Eurozone central banks. He basically said that if Italy, or Greece, or Portugal, or Spain left the Eurozone, then the TARGET2 credits of Germany will not be payable, so it's just paper; they will not be paid if a country were to leave the Eurozone. And the fact is that Germany now has more than 700 billion euros of credit in the TARGET2 system of payments. And it would make sense for Germany to leave the euro in order to have these more than 700 billion euros paid. But they are not doing this, because TARGET2 balances are not credits and are not debts—but Mario Draghi cannot say something different in official statements.

So it's my view, and it's the view also of important economists in the European Union, that there is no sort of bill to be paid by a country leaving the Eurozone.

Gallagher: So in other words, his threat that Italy would have to pay something like 350 or 360 billion euros to Germany if it left the euro—this is an empty

European Commission

European Central Bank President Mario Draghi.

threat, and the German economists themselves know it?

Zanni: It's just European bureaucrats' bullshit—let's describe it that way. [laughter] They usually use this threat in order to get rid of people, or to impose something on the health of millions of citizens that don't want this European Union, that don't want this monetary union, don't want the euro.

Gallagher: But, as you say, at the same time, he was acknowledging for the first time in the letter that the possibility is there for a country or countries to exit from the Union, or exit from the common currency.

Let me ask you, in Italy recently, there have been debates in the parliament on a number of different bills to restore the Glass-Steagall Act? What's the situation with that in Italy?

Zanni: As you said, there are a lot of bills under discussion in the Italian Parliament about restoring Glass-Steagall in Italy. But as you may know, banking regulation in the European Union is decided at the European institutional level. So basically there is the Basel Committee and the Financial Stability Board, where G-20 countries put forward guidelines about banking regulation, and then the European Union legislates concerning new banking regulation.

And I can talk about the situation inside the European institutions. So, we started working on the so-called BSR, Banking Structural Reform—a sort of huge legislative package in the European Union that is supposed to be valid for all the European countries concerning banking separation. So we started, and my group, and myself as shadow rapporteur, supported a sort of new and modern Glass-Steagall legislation, with a strong separation between investment banks and commercial banks, and with a very restricted list of what sort of activities commercial banks can do and what they can purchase.

But the rapporteur, the majority of the European Parliament, and a couple of European countries in the Council decided to block this legislation, so we are stuck with the BSR. After two and a half years, the BSR is on hold at the Council level, so there is no way to have this legislation, this Banking Structural Reform, done, with this majority at the European Union level. So, we hope, as I say, after this wave of general elections that we will have in the European Union in 2017, we will have a majority in the European Council, amongst the European member-states, and in the European Parliament, to start working again on the Banking Structural Reform and to propose this new model for a European Glass-Steagall legislation. That should be done very, very quickly.

Because I would like to underline a statement by the Single Supervisory Mechanism (SSM) chair, the supervisory arm of the ECB, the institution that is supposed to supervise the most important and the biggest banks in the European Union in the banking union; basically, they were asked during that conference about Level three assets, i.e. derivatives holdings of the major European banks—and basically, as I asked of Daniele Nouy, the chair of the SSM in October 2014, they were asked about Level three assets, and basically the reply of the ECB was "we cannot assess the Level Three asset risk because we are not able to evaluate or to decide the value of those instruments, because they are highly speculative instruments, and the regulator is not able to assess the risk of those instruments."

Gallagher: So just to get clear, the ECB announced that it's unable to say what the risk of the derivatives in the European banking system is?

Zanni: What it is, and what is the asset value of these derivatives! So that's really crazy, because the most important banks in Europe, such as Deutsche Bank or HSBC, BNP Paribas and so on, they use inter-nal models in order to establish the value of these illiquid derivatives. So, basically, it is the bank itself that is deciding what is the balance value, the asset value of the derivatives—and the ECB, the institution that should supervise and should control those banks, is clearly stating that they are not able to assess the risk and the value of those instruments.

And let me say that that's really, really crazy. So we should stop banks creating and investing people's money in such an instrument.

Gallagher: And let me ask you about—you mentioned earlier, Italian banks, specifically *Monte dei Paschi* bank, which is a bank that as I understand it, was basically ruined by derivatives, which it bought; what is the condition of the Italian banking system you started to talk about, and the relationship to the other banks in Europe to that?

Zanni: Basically the Italian banking system has failed. I estimated that we need more than 60 billion euros of fresh capital in order to recapitalize the Italian banking system. The government and the European Union are ignoring these needs; they are talking about a disastrous bail-in; they are talking about using private money to bail-in the banks; they are talking about "market solutions," but all the market solutions proposed by the ECB and by the Italian government, failed. So a sort of private recapitalization, with a sort of public offering of new shares for Monte dei Paschi failed at the end of 2016, because there were no investors that were able to put money in the banks. Now they are talking about a public intervention in Monte dei Paschi, but the problem is not only Monte dei Paschi, but is the entire Italian banking system.

And as I said before, I estimated that we need more than 60 billion euros—at least! more than 60 billion euros—in order to be recapitalized.

But if we recapitalize the Italian banking system and we continue to have this system without banking separation, without regulation of derivatives and of risky assets, then in five years we will be at the same level and at the same point, asking our citizens for money in order to bail out banks.

So, we need, in the short term, to recapitalize our banks, and only the government could have the huge amount of money required to do it. But in the medium and long term, we need new banking legislation, starting from a sort of new Glass-Steagall legislation, in order to strictly regulate our banks. That's the only way to save our country. That's the only way to save our banking system, and thus the savings of Italian families and Italian SMEs.

Gallagher: Basically what you're proposing then that has to be done in Italy, is both a recapitalization of these banks and also a Glass-Steagall separation—and what then for the Italian economy? Do you have an idea how it can recover?

Zanni: I think that the only way that the Italian economy can recover is to leave the euro, leave the European Union and the absurdity of their rules. Leave the so-called Maastricht conditions, the 3% public deficit/GDP ratio, the 60% public debt/GDP ratio, the public bonds balance sheet, and all these anti-economic rules. If we want to regain, or to have a strong economic recovery in Italy, an improvement in the condition of salaries and income for Italian citizens, we need get rid of those rules of the single currency, to regain our power to control our central banks. And my view is that we have to finance recovery through a monetization of our debts—a sort of liquidity provided by the central bank to the central government. We have to set up a huge infrastructural investment plan in order to restart the Italian economy.

I'm looking with huge interest at what the so-called BRICS, the emerging economies of Asia are doing in this field, with the Asian Infrastructure Investment Bank, with the project of One Belt, One Road supported by the Chinese and Russian governments, with other emerging countries supporting it. So I think we need this kind of investment approach in Italy. A huge investment plan in infrastructure, in the green economy, in a lot of sectors, financed by the central bank. That's the only way ahead. And we can do it only outside the European Union and outside the Eurozone.

Gallagher: You were in the United States in the summer of 2015, working on these objectives, particularly the Glass-Steagall Act in both the United States and Europe. You met with Congressional staffs and some members of Congress in both Houses. So you have an insight into that. What do you look for in the United States, now?

Zanni: It's very difficult to see what the new administration will do about Glass-Steagall. Looking at what Mr. Trump said, he probably supports the sort of new banking regulation that could comprehend also, banking separation and restoring the Glass-Steagall Act. But

Creative Commons/Pava

"The only way that the Italian economy can recover is to leave the euro, leave the European Union and the absurdity of their rules."

at the same time, I'm looking at the fact that in a lot of top, senior positions, he's hiring former investment bankers coming from Goldman Sachs and other investment banks.

Also, the majority of the Republican Congressmen, probably, do not support restoring Glass-Steagall. But if Mr. Trump is convinced that the United States needs a new banking reform—basically sort of a new U.S. Glass-Steagall—I think he can very, very quickly and very, very easily push the Congress, the Republican Party, and all of his staff in order to work on this kind of reform.

When I was in D.C. last year, it was very important to me to show how the effect of bad banking regulation could be dangerous for an economy. I showed the example of Italy and of the European Union. So, I asked the U.S. Congressmen and Congresswomen that I met in 2016, to review the Dodd-Frank Act, your banking regulation, because it is very dangerous. There is a provisional bail-in rule also in your Dodd-Frank banking legislation. The effects of the bail-in on the European banking system have been very, very dangerous.

If you look at the share price of Deutsche Bank, for example, or of Italian banks, the share price for those banks dropped by, on average, more than 70% from the moment—from January 2016—when the bail-in rule took effect in the European Union. This rule is very dangerous. You have this rule in Dodd-Frank. It has never been applied, but it could be at any moment, so I think that you need to review the Dodd-Frank legislation.

And I think if Mr. Trump pushes for this, he can have the support also of a huge part of the Democratic Party, of Bernie Sanders, and a lot of Congressmen and Congresswomen that I met during my visit to DC.

Gallagher: Well, I should just tell you that La-Rouche PAC currently is in a national petition-drive; apparently the first address that Trump makes to the Joint Session of Congress is going to be Feb. 28th: We're in a national petition-drive calling on him to promise and propose Glass-Steagall to that session of Congress on the 28th of February, just one month away. And Lyndon LaRouche has also called for the rejection of the nomination of Steven Mnuchin, one of those whom you referred to, who's been nominated for Treasury Secretary, and in his confirmation came out bluntly against Glass-Steagall, despite the fact that the questioner was reminding him that the President who nominated him had promised Glass-Steagall restoration in the campaign. So we are also, and LaRouche has called for him to be rejected and kept out of the Treasury.

So if there's anything further that you want to get across to people watching this station here in particular, go ahead.

Zanni: Just one last thing, is it is very good news to know about this petition that you are bringing forward in the United States, because the support of civil society is very important in pushing politicians to pass the right legislation about the banks and banking regulation.

What about Europe and what the new U.S. administration—a sort of next step? I hope that the approach that the new U.S. administration is bringing forward towards Europe and the European Union, would be very positive for Italy. In order to exit the euro, we need the support of the United States, and we need the support also of Russia. So it's very important that the new cooperative approach that Mr. Trump has with Mr. Putin, with Russia, and with other emerging economies, would have a positive impact in destroying this European Union, and rebuilding Europe—a Europe based on sovereignty, and a Europe based on free nations, and a cooperative Europe that could work well and could cooperate with the United States from one side, and Russia and the Asian region from the other side. So we need both sides of the world, and thus the United States and Russia, in order to get rid of this imperialist project that is the European Union.

So I hope that Mr. Trump will maintain this approach which is very critical, this very critical approach that he has with the European Union, with Germany, and with the euro, and could help Italy exit the euro, and could help Europe rebuild a new history—a sort of new framework that is based on more cooperation, on more economic growth and on more jobs and investment. And that's my hope and that's my appeal to the new U.S. administration.

Gallagher: Great. Okay, we've been talking just for the last half-hour with Marco Zanni, a Member of the European Parliament from Italy. I want to thank you, Marco, very much for having really imparted a great deal in the short time that we've been on, and I hope to talk to you again very soon.

This is Paul Gallagher signing off for LaRouche PAC TV.

IV. Lyndon LaRouche, in 2011, Forecast the End of the British Empire

BERWICK, BLAIR, HITLER & OBAMA:

The Death of London's Roman Empire

by Lyndon H. LaRouche, Jr.

January 10, 2011

In earlier published reports, I had warned, in one way or another, that the Roman empire, which is represented presently by the terminal conditions of the hyper-inflated British empire, has reached the fag end of its tyrannies, in one manner or another. Either the British empire will be shut down soon, or the entire planet were presently at the brink of its collapse into a prolonged, global nightmare, a new "Dark Age" far worse than that which Europe experienced during the 14th Century.

However, it were true, hypothetically, that the United Kingdom itself could survive this threat, and the world at large, too; but, that could occur only if the United Kingdom were induced to abandon what Rosa Luxemburg[1], and also the U.S. State Department's historian Herbert Feis[2], had identified correctly as the systemic form of what, in fact, was the British empire as such. I supplement Feis's studies with the fact that the British empire is still, at this moment, an empire which is, in fact, the current expression of that imperialism which was originally that of the monetarist form of empire launched by the then future Caesar Augustus on the Isle of Capri.

The original Roman empire passed through a succession of crises, sometimes as the Roman Empire by name, sometimes as Byzantium, sometimes as the system of Nietzschean-like "creative destruction" under the old Venetian monetarist system, sometimes as that New Venetian system led by Paolo Sarpi, which became known as the Anglo-Dutch imperialist system, and, now, since the assassination of U.S. President John F. Kennedy and the U.S. folly of a long Indo-China war, the presently crashing world empire associated with that so-called "BRIC" based on Lord Jacob Rothschild's folly known as the presently crashing Inter-Alpha Group.

Unless that hopelessly bankrupt Inter-Alpha Group is mercifully buried, pre-emptively, now, the planet as a whole will be plunged into the doom represented by an end of all successive phases of the existence of the Roman Empire, from its founding on the Isle of Capri, to the present days.

The only efficient way to explain the process at work, is to identify the principle which was presented, from the top down, in the crafting of the great principle on which the Preamble of the original U.S. Federal Constitution is premised to the present day. That is the same principle which is better known today as the Glass-Steagall principle—known as a name, but rarely, competently understood. I explain.

Foreword:

The Roman Empire

There has been, recently, a foolish tradition in the writing of history, and I am referring here, chiefly to the history of the trans-Atlantic world preceding and during the history of the Mediterranean region, up through the

---

1. **The Accumulation of Capital**, Chapter 30, "International Loans," 1913.
2. **Europe The World's Banker 1870-1914** (New Haven: Yale University Press, 1930).

present time. It is a tradition of viewing such phenomena as persons, generations, and even entire national cultures, each as discrete objects interacting, as if kinematically, among themselves, rather than, properly, as a continuing process of cosmic-like development, within which singularities appear as products of the continuing interactions within the trans-generational processes which are any real historical process.

Thus, to illustrate the just-stated point, consider the deep roots of all globally extended European history, with regard for its influence on the planet more widely, as this is traceable from the ironies of what are identified as Classical Greek roots, from the Homeric accounts onward.

That said, as a matter of forewarning, what we, today call "Greece" participated in the defeat of the Achaemenid Empire in the end, but, nonetheless, that ancient Greece, self-cursed by the Delphi cult which it had trusted all too much, had already destroyed itself with the folly of the Peloponnesian War, and would never become an empire, as Robert Burns would say, "For all that."

Macedon's Prince Philip, whose own folly had set him up to be killed, thus left the throne in the hand of Philip's son and adversary, Alexander the Great. In the end of all that, Aristotle, the poisoner, triumphed in the death of Alexander. Thus, the attempt at an empire of the maritime power of the Mediterranean would wait until the completion of the negotiations, conducted on the Isle of Capri, between that tyrant Octavian who was the murderer of the Cicero who had been the only real hero for Shakespeare's **Julius Caesar** tragedy, between the Octavian actually known as the then future Caesar Augustus, and the priests of the cult of Mithra.

In such a manner, the Roman Empire emerged as an imperial maritime form of world empire centered, originally, on the Mediterranean, which it became, and has remained of late, as the British Empire, since the day William of Orange had invaded, and largely raped the British Isles, all done under the invader's flag of Paolo Sarpi's "New Venetian" empire, thus initiating what became the British Empire as the world's reigning monetarist power, still today.

So, with the decline of Rome, the leading oligarchical families of Rome had fled to the brack-ish swamps at the north of the Adriatic, to emerge, again, from amid a then-decaying Byzantium, as the reigning imperial monetarist body of the same old Roman Empire from approximately A.D. 1000, until the present day under the direction of the Venetian monetarists' nominally British monetarist system of imperialism. Venice, in turn, under Paolo Sarpi, transformed itself from the Aristotelean form which had been traditional since the time of the elimination of Plato, into a

As with the Roman Empire, which collapsed in the 5th Century, today's hyperinflated British Empire has reached the fag end of its tyrannies. Either it will soon disappear, or the entire planet will sink into a prolonged, global nightmare, a new "Dark Age." Shown: "Rome: Ruins of the Forum, Looking towards the Capitol," by Canaletto, 1742.

modified form of "The New Venice," that of the followers of modern Europe's Paolo Sarpi, thus defining the process leading from the utterly depraved Venetian puppet which was the English monarchy of Henry VIII, into the late Sixteenth-century degeneracy of Marlowe's and Shakespeare's England under the flag of Paolo Sarpi's doctrine of "Liberalism."

So, betwixt the invasion of the British Isles by William of Orange's Sarpian "New Venetian Party," and today, the last gasp of the old Roman Empire is to be found in the onrushing, self-inflicted doom of the old Roman Empire as the present British Empire of Lord Jacob Rothschild's hopelessly worthless Inter-Alpha Group, the swindle also known as "The BRIC."

The outcome of that set of pages of the world history of modern, trans-Atlantic civilization, is that the entire world is, presently, gripped systemically, by the presently continuing conflict between two leading cultures, the monetarist culture of a Europe presently dominated by the tyranny of the British Empire, versus the culture of a credit-system founded in North America over the interval from the establishment of the Massachusetts Bay Colony under the leadership of the Winthrops and Mathers. It was the consequent, later founding of the United States as a constitutional republic, as defined by the Preamble of its Federal Constitution, which was echoed by the miraculous resuscitation of that great republic under such exemplary Presidents as Abraham Lincoln, and in President Franklin Delano Roosevelt's crucial role in launching of the Glass-Steagall Law.

Presently, unless that 1933 Glass-Steagall Law were immediately re-established, now, the continued existence of the United States were soon ended in a bloody, hyper-inflationary collapse now nearing its end. There is no action by the U.S. President and U.S. Congress which is "worth a hill of beans," unless the re-enactment and enforcement of that Glass-Steagall Law occurs as a foremost priority now.

The problem is, that unless this current U.S. President were ejected, as might be done under the relevant provisions of Section 4 of the U.S. 25th Amendment to the Constitution, the continued existence of the United States is not possible by any known, lawful means under its own law. There is, therefore, no other morally tolerable commitment by the institutions of our Federal government, than the two-fold measure of immediately re-enacting the 1933 Glass-Steagall Law, and ending the power of the current President to prevent the prompt and efficient re-installation of that 1933 Glass-Steagall law.

Abandon all silly chatter about worthless hopes for rescue by a general U.S. election approximately two years ahead; under present trends, a new election under our Constitution would probably never occur. Without Glass-Steagall, the United States will soon cease to exist in any presently recognizable form, if it exists in any form at all, even past the relatively few months now immediately ahead. A state of global, hyper-inflationary collapse, is already built into the trans-Atlantic system. The count-down to doom is already on, unless we replace Obama now.

The Global Outlook

Without the type of reform which I prescribe here, the trans-Atlantic economy and its nations are already as much as foredoomed to rot; I present the summary proof of that fact within these pages. Whereas Asia's problems are not hopeless in themselves, but tend toward a contrary, and, therefore, happier direction, a collapse of several leading economies of Asia, which would occur as an echo of any collapse of the trans-Atlantic system, would carry all of Asia down with it. You can blame Lord Jacob Rothschild's system, which he installed, *circa* 1971 as part of the treasonous intention of the London-directed U.S.A.'s abandoning of the Bretton Woods System, an implicitly treasonous, August 1971 change, introduced as an alternative to the U.S.A.'s fixed-exchange-rate system which had been established by President Franklin Roosevelt's triumph over John Maynard Keynes at Bretton Woods. A presently inevitable, already ongoing collapse of the Inter-Alpha system and its auxiliaries, would presently bring down the entire world economic system, chain-reaction style.

Without immediate re-enactment of President Franklin Roosevelt's Glass-Steagall action of 1933, the planet as a whole were soon plunged into the deepest, widest, and longest dark age in historic times.

Thus, the doom of the British stage of the Roman empire lies, now, not in the hands of its present adversaries, but, finally, in no other foe as much as itself.

The ancient, and continuing root of the combination of already existing or immediately threatened, global disaster, lies, essentially, in the concept of **monetarism** itself, in the delusory obscenity of the belief that money as such represents a rational standard of "economic value." Hence, for as long as the nations are intoxicated by belief in the folly of monetarists' systems, the present situation of the nations of the planet as a whole, even any form of belief prevalent as the ruling sentiment of the most influential laws of mankind as a whole, were presently a hopeless case.

Contrary to the monetarists, all of whom have now failed as would-be professionals, I am a physical economist in the same tradition as the authors of our U.S. Republic and the great principle set forth in the Preamble of our Federal Constitution to which all representatives of our Federal government have sworn a solemn oath of allegiance, whether they either meant what they have said, or whether they had, or had not known the actual significance of what they had merely said.[3]

Therefore, I summarize the truthful scientific principle of economy in those terms of historical and physical-scientific reference, here, as follows.

Library of Congress

*Britain is a maritime form of empire, LaRouche writes, an international dictatorship imposed upon a collection of otherwise, ostensibly separate nations, as seen in the post-Westphalian, euro system today. This 1902 **Puck** cartoon depicts "Britannia," as "Civilization" crushing the "Barbarians."*

I. What Is the British Empire?

The British empire, which has never been understood by more than a handful of modern economists, such as Rosa Luxemburg and the U.S. State Department historian and scholar Herbert Feis, has now entered what will soon turn out to have become the last gasp of its existence, that in one way or another. Either the British empire, a maritime empire, is soon wiped from the map, or, in the alternative, the effort to maintain the existence of that inherently failed empire will send the entirety of the planet to Hell for a long time to come.

The effect of the resumed influence of the British empire over the policies of the United States, has progressively ruined us since the death of President Franklin Roosevelt, especially since the successful assassination of a President John F. Kennedy which broke President Kennedy's and General Douglas MacArthur's resistance to entering the British trap for the

United States which the British empire had crafted in Indo-China. The Kennedy assassination, thus, unleashed ten years of physical and moral ruin of the institutions and people of the United States from which our republic has not yet returned, still today.

Such a maritime form of empire as that which the British empire exerts over Europe today, is the expression of an international dictatorship imposed upon a collection of otherwise, ostensibly separate nations, exactly as the "Post-Westphalian" policy of the present, so-called "Post-Westphalian," "Euro" system prescribes today. The quality of the Roman empire and its relevant sequels, as expressed by the British empire today, has two most essential characteristics, as follows.

The first characteristic of that empire, is that of an imperial "personality" with the power to decree a body of international law, presently termed "governance," imposed upon all subject "kingdoms." It is a power which lies in the personal authority of the Emperor, such as, nominally the British monarchy, as the body which functions as the *de jure* person of the emperor to equivalent effect. Such is the presently attempted form of the British empire's tyranny against the nations of continental Europe, since the imposition of the "Euro" system of monetarist imperialism by the concerted action against Germany by Britain's Margaret Thatcher, France's President François Mitterrand, and U.S. President George H.W. Bush, in 1990 and beyond. Similarly,

---

3. There are professional economists whose work I applaud on many accounts, but my own successes as a forecaster, since the 1950s, are unrivaled, while my skills as a physical economist have been, on the record so far, unique.

earlier, the intended design of Adolf Hitler's imperial form of Reich, had been a system of a form inhering in the British intention for the Euro system today. Such was the kindred import of the implicitly treasonous "signing statements" uttered against the Federal Constitution of the United States itself, under U.S. Presidents George W. Bush, Jr. and Barack Obama.

Second, all empires of that sort, are contained within a monetarist system which operates, through international institutions, as an imperial authority, as the design of the Euro system, essentially by the British crown, prescribes this condition for the "governance" of its victims, its subjects, presently.

Such systems are typified by examples such as the original Roman Empire, by Byzantium, by the extended Norman system under the direction of Venetian monetarism, by Sarpi's pre-shaping of the so-called "Liberalism" of the British empire, and by the expanded British Empire which dominates, and loots the Euro system presently.

For deeper insight into the Europe-based forms of such imperial tyrannies, one must examine the root of this system in the role of the Delphi cult in its time. The affirmation of "the oligarchical principle" by agreement between Macedon's King Philip and the Achaemenid empire, illustrates the point. Aristotle, like, later, that high priest of Delphi from the Roman empire's reign, Plutarch, remains a notable, ancient exponent of that oligarchical system of evil presently.

It is the currently, frankly expressed intention of the British empire, to bring about the early destruction of our United States. That treasonous effort is being done by the relevant "Wall Street" financier interests, through aid of the complicity of the present, increasingly Hitler-like health-care and related policies of the current U.S. Obama administration. That administration is working to make the way clear for an unchallenged world-empire whose intended center would be the British power in the City of London's reign over the former continental nations of Europe. Hence, the implicitly treasonous role of the British puppet-President of the United States, Barack Obama, in clearing the way for an imperial system of "world government" under a so-called "post-Westphalian system," as a system under which national sovereignties are outlawed by the replacement of government (i.e., premised on the "consent of the governed") by a "post-Westphalian" imperialism's system of "governance."

As under the system of the Delphi maritime cult and of the Roman Empire, alike, the essence of the empire is its "supra-national" system of rule under a supra-national, monetarist system such as that established by the U.S. Nixon Administration's repeal of the fixed-exchange rate: an international money-system which rules, as an oligarchical social system, among and over nations, and which represents a reign maintained through the promotion of an imperial form of monetarist authority located among nations, rather than within any among them. Such is the intrinsically imperialistic, intrinsically treasonous character of what is called "governance."

In general, since the establishment of the Roman Empire, with relatively rarer, and relatively short-term exceptions, the European system has been a collection of "kingdoms" under the imperial rule of a trans-national, monetarist system. That has been the issue of the essential distinction of the constitutional system of the U.S.A. from the long trend in European systems thus far.

The U.S. Constitution's Great Principle

The great struggle of all humanity presently, is a struggle of nation-states to secure their freedom from the looting practices of a presently dying world system, that of the British monetarist empire in its present form. Since that empire is systemically a monetarist system, the comprehension of the great existential struggle for a return to a system of freedom, depends upon the enforcement of a global, fixed-exchange-rate system modeled on the great fundamental principle of constitutional law expressed as the Preamble of the U.S.A. Federal Constitution.

From the outset of the preparation and installation of that Federal Constitution based on that great principle of its Preamble, our republic has been premised on the same notion of a credit-system, rather than a monetarist system, a credit-system which was pioneered under the sovereignty assured by the original Royal Charter of the Massachusetts Bay Colony and the colony's Pine Tree Shilling-based credit-system.

Under that tradition, and the Constitution created to establish that principle as a sovereign nation-state system, our United States had been the only durable expression of a truly sovereign nation-state within a world over which the Roman empire in its British incarnation had reigned, with few and brief exceptions, since the devastation wrought by the French Revolution and its recurring victimization by the British Empire which had been implicitly established in the February 1763

Peace of Paris.

All major warfare on this planet since that 1763 Peace of Paris, has been the expression of an imperial practice of attempted dictatorial management of this entire planet through monetarist practices aided by recurring long wars, including the perpetually recurring state of such ruinously long, intentionally geopolitical wars on this planet as those launched by the British empire through the effects of the British monarchy's ouster of Germany's Chancellor Bismarck, in 1890, as, also, recently, under the same British Prime Minister Tony Blair who has revived the criminal health-care policies of the Adolf Hitler regime in the United Kingdom and, now, under the British-appointed puppet-President of our United States, Barack Obama, presently.

To regain the constitutional order prescribed in the Federal Constitution of our republic, we must first regain an insight into those great principles of our republic which have suffered infraction against our constitutional principle through acts expressing an imperialist enemy's hatred of our republic, an enemy who has been determined to destroy the great principle of our republic ever since the time of the 1763 Peace of Paris. The great issue which has been the recurring source of mortal struggles between our patriots and the British monetarist system, as since the time of that 1763 Peace of Paris, has been our republic's recurring return to the affirmation of the principle of a credit-system, rather than that imperialist system of monetarism, as the monetarist system is expressed for our United States by the implicitly treasonous character of the once Hitler-loving Wall Street of Brown Brothers Harriman, which was the type of a usurious predator which makes slaves of all those who become its victims.

Only the affirmation of the principle of a credit-system, rather than a monetarist system, as the original Glass-Steagall Law expresses that U.S. Constitutional principle, could now prevent the entirety of this planet from an early plunge into a global Hell from which civilization would not recover for many generations to come. To this end, the institutions and citizens of our United States must clear the cobwebs of the rabid, pleasure-pain-driven irrationalism of the Paolo Sarpi-Adam Smith liberalism from their minds, to see, and obey that true principle of the credit system which is inherent in the founding of our republic and its Federal Constitution.

II. The Science of Physical Economy

The most essential of the preconditions for the political freedom which our Federal Constitution was intended to secure for us and our posterity, is the commitment to an increase in the net *physical* powers of productivity of the means of existence of a growing population of our republic, and, hopefully, a contribution of a kindred quality for other nations as well. On this account, there can be no other definition of wealth than *the net increase* of the physical wealth produced per capita and per square kilometer of territory of our nation, and, also, our assistance to that same quality of end for the other nations with which our republic must cooperate, that done for common ends, on behalf of the general welfare of humanity as a whole.

It is the nature of the universe, a nature which must be the guidance of all sane nations and their peoples, that our universe demands, as a condition for our survival, that we pursue a vigorously anti-entropic policy of universal practice, as, for the case of "fire," which only mankind among all living creatures, practices, through a persistent increase in the energy-flux-density in the principal forms of action on which not only the progress, but the very survival of a human culture depends.

So, survival of mankind exists, presently, only in a vigorous advance into the increased power to exist of an age defined by nuclear fission and thermonuclear fusion, and beyond, exactly as the history of the emergence of, and progress in life on Earth has always depended, so far, and will depend, increasingly in the decades immediately ahead.

The currently onrushing great general economic-breakdown crisis, has been, in a large degree, the increasingly contrary, and increasingly fatal error of belief and practice among our citizens and the institutions of government which is called "monetarism," "monetary theory," and such. In short, the conflict between President Franklin Roosevelt and John Maynard Keynes, during the proceedings of the 1944 Bretton Woods conference.

The trouble was, that soon after that, President Franklin Roosevelt died, to be succeeded by a Vice-President Harry S Truman who had been a Wall Street Democratic Party crony of fascist-leaning implications, and, also, a bit of a late-comer in recognizing the nature of the evil of those combined British and Wall

The continued survival of mankind exists depends upon the vigorous advance of an increase in power, as defined by nuclear fission and thermonuclear fusion. Shown: Sandia National Laboratories' "Z Machine," the world's largest X-ray generator, which, it is hoped, will, one day, ignite a nuclear fusion reaction.

Street financier interests, such as the head of the Bank of England and his partner, Brown Brothers Harriman, which had, in fact, brought Adolf Hitler to power in Germany.

Already, once the Allied forces, led by General Dwight Eisenhower, had effected the successful landing in Normandy, the same old "American Tory" attachment was resumed as the expression of Franklin Roosevelt haters whose loyalties had lain between those British imperialist interests and their Wall Street cronies who, as in the case of Brown Brothers Harriman and its official Prescott Bush, had funded bringing Adolf Hitler into power in Germany. The British intelligence service's role in the wrecking of the surrender being prepared by relevant German generals, and the seemingly insane Montgomery-led caper of the First Army, successfully postponed the gaining of the Allied victory for virtually another year, during which many Americans in service, and others, died. With the death of President Franklin Roosevelt, and the accession of

the Wall Street-friendly Harry S Truman, the cause of our United States suffered a defeat from which we have never fully recovered as a nation, to the present day—despite great Presidents such as the Dwight Eisenhower and the John F. Kennedy who operated under hostile and also, especially for President Kennedy and his brother, implicitly deadly conditions.

Thus, the time came, when the assassination of President Kennedy had plunged the United States into the long, foolish war in Indo-China, from which our United States has never resumed its true self, to the present day.

So, in these and like ways, most among our lawful and other political leaders, have lost a large part of the essential moral and intellectual inclination which was specific to the founding of what was to become our republic in Seventeenth-century Massachusetts, and in the great achievements under our greatest elected and other leaders during sundry periods of the Eighteenth and Nineteenth centuries, as, also, under a

President Franklin Roosevelt whose conscience inherited the devotion of an ancestor, Isaac Roosevelt, who had been allied with the designer of our U.S. constitutional economic policy, Treasury Secretary Alexander Hamilton.

We had also been led, in a good time, by a President Franklin Roosevelt whose comprehension of our great Constitutional principle is virtually unknown among most of those newly elected members of the U.S. Congress today, who, if allowed, will destroy what remains of our republic, members of the Congress who, today, proceed, in large part, with brutish lack of comprehension of the nature of their own incompetence. How could a man swear an oath to perform a duty of which he has no comprehension?

Today, there is presently virtually no comprehension of the actuality of those great principles on which the unique genius of our republic had depended thus far. Without re-educating much of our republic's political leadership, and citizens alike, by giving them back the great principles understood by those, such as the Winthrops and Mathers, who planted the roots of our great American design, there is little likelihood that either our republic, or any part of the world's civilization at large, will survive the increasingly terrible months now just ahead.

Presently, most of the trans-Atlantic world's leaders, and ordinary folk, too, have a gambler's instinctive wish for good luck, rather than relying upon scientifically valid principles. They cast dice with little reason, and hate the most, any person who doubts the infallibility of their desperate, and wretchedly failed ambition. When doom descends upon them, they whine: "They should not have let this happen to me. You must bail me out, whatever it might cost you, even the very life of the members of your family!"

To get down to fundamentals, respecting my numerous achievements as a forecaster, contrary to that of notable other specialists in the field, the difference between my successful method of forecasting and analysis, and their usually failed foresights, has been, essentially, ontological: Their forecasts are premised on a statistical (e.g., *phenomenological*) standpoint (statistics, the Sarpian, "touchy-feely" Liberalism of Adam Smith), whereas mine are *ontological* (physical principles). The most publicized example of this difference, is that reflected in my defeat of a leading British economist of the intrinsically pro-fascist tradition of the cult of "creative destruction" of such as Friedrich

Nietzsche, Werner Sombart, Joseph Schumpeter, and the likes of Larry Summers: the Professor Abba Lerner whom I defeated in a celebrated New York's Queens College debate on December 2, 1971.

Instead of those prevalent, but essentially incompetent notions of principles of political-economy, we must consider economy as not statistical monetarism, but as being at the core of the principles of a human practice of a physical science.

Economy as Physical Science

Contrary to the poor fellows who had lately come to occupy precious positions of government and the like, any distinctively competent form of a physical science of economy for today, is essentially a reflection of the current of physical science coherent with two of the greatest scientific geniuses of recent centuries, Bernard Riemann and the Academician V.I. Vernadsky who was no Marxist, but a patriot of Russia who performed his mission of devotion to both Russia and Ukraine, and, to humanity at large, as well.

For the purpose of an adequate appreciation of the relevance of Vernadsky's leading contributions to a less imperfect science of physical economy, still today, we must recognize the crucial role which the work of physicist Bernhard Riemann had contributed in defining the conceptual foundations for all of those most singular achievements which were either contributed by Vernadsky, or expressed a shared world-outlook respecting not only science, but on mankind as such, an outlook, which, despite those statisticians who seem to trace their intellectual ancestry to Jonathan Swift's floating island of Laputa, permeates still all of the greatest of the surviving achievements of science in the world at large still today.

Apart from the fact, that I have been an extraordinarily, even often, uniquely successful physical-economic forecaster since my first such success in 1956-7, all of my own significant contributions to any actually competent notion of a physical science of economy, have been, essentially, a product of the interrelationship between my own knowledge of a physical-economic process as such, and the foundations, in the fundamental contributions of Riemann, for appreciating what I later came to recognize as the indispensable function, for a competent science of economy, of Vernadsky's rigorous treatment of the respective and interdependent notions of the *lithosphere*, *biosphere*, and *noösphere*.

Thus, competent economic science, is physical-economic science, not statistical forecasting. It has nothing to do with the likes of such charlatans as both that pair of dupes of Bertrand Russell, the John von Neumann and Professor Norbert Wiener whom David Hilbert had tossed out of the faculty at Göttingen. More to the point, recently accumulated investigations bearing on the leading role of what is termed a "cosmic radiation" permeating what is never, and nowhere a part of "empty space," now depend on deeper insight into the conclusive quality and forward-looking implications of the apparent qualitative divisions, and interrelations among the *lithosphere,*

Recent investigations bearing on the role of cosmic radiation "permeating what is never, and nowhere a part of 'empty space,' now depend on deeper insight into the conclusive quality and forward-looking implications of the apparent qualitative divisions, and interrelations among the Lithosphere, Biosphere, and Noösphere," within our galaxy. Shown: "Aurora Borealis," by Frederic Edwin Church, 1865.

biosphere, and noösphere within the confines of that region which our Solar system inhabits on our galaxy's periphery.

In addition to what relevant physical-science professionals have brought to us, as such, my own leading work concerning the human mind, intersects those considerations in a crucial way. The most relevant implication of these considerations, is the proof of the falseness of the naive notion of "sense-certainty," a proof which shows us that the human mind's true function is that mind's direct relationship to the universe, as ancient, trans-oceanic maritime cultures from no later than the last great ice age, already anticipated, in practice, the Kepler-Einstein principle of trans-oceanic navigation, that the universe of the stellar navigational system's star-map, is finite, but not bounded.[4]

The unique success of Johannes Kepler in defining the Mars and Earth solar orbits in his **New Astronomy**, and his subsequent, uniquely original discovery of a principle of gravitation, in his **Harmonies,** point out to us the significance of what Kepler himself defines as a method of "vicarious hypothesis," a discov-

4. Not the silly Titius-Bode concoction of the reductionists' schools.

ery of the ancient Platonic method, and that of Nicholas of Cusa, which assumes its momentous character in the uniqueness of Kepler's discovery of the principle of gravitation. Hence, Einstein's genius in insight into the explicit notion of a universe as finite but not bounded.

Similarly, for most of that time which we can presently attribute to the existence of manifest forms of life on our planet Earth, the evidence has been, that life had been long expressed, chiefly, in something approximating unicellular forms of animal and vegetable life. Thus, for most of what we consider as relevant fossil resources, known human societies have depended upon the accumulation of the massed dead bodies of unicellular, or comparable forms of life.

The development of life itself on Earth, has been the notable cause of the changes in the environment of the planet and its surface, changes which have, in turn, made possible the emergence of higher forms of life. The development of the function of oxygen for life, thus led to the consequent development of the new functional phase-space for life-forms, known as that "ozone layer" which provides the protection needed for higher forms of life. This presents me and my associates in scientific researches with two phase-spaces, each of which has its own characteristics for the way in which life is organized on this planet during the course of the evolutionary development of the respective "platforms."

Such is a fair description of the matter to be considered. The case of iron ores is an illustration.

Most of the raw materials on which civilization depends today are found in fossil remains, such as iron deposits, left behind by deceased forms of what had been living processes. Thus, when we gather up and employ "iron ores," we are depleting the density of the forms of ores left behind by long-deceased expressions of life concentrated in certain environments in this manner. Hence, to overcome the loss of richness of such resources left behind, we must act in ways which have the effect of increasing the equivalent of "the energy-flux density" of the sources of heat-power applied to production for human needs. This pattern of proceeding from raw materials and heat-processes of relatively lower, to higher orders of energy-flux density, has been the basis for every case of a society's ability to maintain its population's ability to maintain an improved, or even a constant level of potential relative population density.

Only the scientifically insane could believe, today, in the outright fraud of presuming that the degeneration of the productive powers of labor by reliance on such wasteful nonsense as windmills and "solar collectors" is allegedly sane policies of practice.

Mankind's willful progress in the discovery and use of heat-sources of relevant forms of higher degrees of energy-flux density, is the precondition for maintaining a viable form of human culture at a pre-existing level. Today, the use of the sources of power such as nuclear fission, and of thermonuclear fusion, have become a growing ration of the indispensable means of rising standards of "energy-flux density" which are, more and more, indispensable for preventing a society's physical and moral degeneracy through attritional processes.

Not only must society rely upon increases in the level of energy-flux densities controlled and employed; mankind must organize the environment by aid of revolutionary transformations of society's cultures to higher levels of the equivalent of energy-flux density.

There is no sane excuse today, for what are the actually mass-homicidal practices of what are called "green" anti-nuclear policies and the like today.

For reasons related to such considerations as those, a competent practice of the principles of economy depends upon discarding virtually everything usually taught as "economics" in common practice of economists and related others today. Therefore, we should not find ourselves surprised, to learn that a competent practice of economics as a science, takes us into what is, in fact, the most profound, and least well known of all presently known branches of physical science. The principle of "energy-flux density," is among the simplest of those often neglected considerations.

It is mankind's tendency to recognize crucial qualities of proof respecting those universal physical principles which are specifically accessible to the development of the processes of the human mind, which defines an implicitly direct relationship between the creative powers innately developable in the human mind and the universe with which that mind is interacting. It is man's conception of that relationship between ourselves, our cultural progress, as in science, and the universe which man inhabits, which is the basis for anything of truthful value which man can adduce for lowered ontological forms of existence.

To proceed from that broad overview of man in the universe, to the preconditions for man's overcoming the forces of attrition, we must consider some among the most important of the relatively simpler of the physical-scientific considerations. I begin the series of considerations to be taken into account, by explaining my objections to the continuing use of the term "infrastructure."

III. The Allusion to 'Infrastructure'

I have, recently, discarded further use of the term "infrastructure" as a term of professional economics. Instead, I have introduced the term "platforms," as notions to free me of the popular, but imprecise meaning of the term "environment." There have been several crucial considerations.

I shall approach the subject of these platforms, in two, successive ways. First, I shall indicate the terms to be used as definitions of certain, pivotal technical terms used for this purpose. Second, I shall restate the case in terms describing an actually historical process which represents the modern cultural roots of the existence of our United States. The significance of those notions, is that they correspond to the character of space-time relations within both the planet and its particular regions, rather than being typical of the limits of an occurrence of a specific localized action.

Therefore, I begin this chapter with the included subject of the *transport* functions listed in historical, or quasi-historical orderings: water (maritime); water (riparian/rivers integrated with canals—as under Charlemagne); railway systems; high-speed transcontinental railway systems; very-high-speed track (rail or maglev) systems; ultra-high speed systems (e.g. 1000 mph in semi-evacuated tubes); and, extra-terrestrial systems.

Next, we have to consider the chemical infrastructure treated in terms of technological levels of "power," as defined, chiefly, in "levels" of energy-flux-density, as expressed by the modal physical chemistry of society's general, or local practice. This includes the role, since ancient times, of that notion of the general use of "fire" which is presently known as a characteristic behavior unique to mankind among all known living species, "fire" as to be measured by us, here, in units of "relative energy-flux density."

Next, we have the quality of intellectual cultural level of development of mankind within society considered as an ongoing process. E.g.: "Classical artistic" and "scientific" education of the population generally (as an expression of the intellectual potential which is characteristic of a specific quality of a human population). Putting this in relevant, other terms, this means the general intellectual development of power expressed intellectually by the culture of a nation or comparable society; this points to a general intellectual level of a national or comparable division of culture, as distinguished, as an underlying category of aptitude of a culture, as *a notion of potential*, as contrasted to the

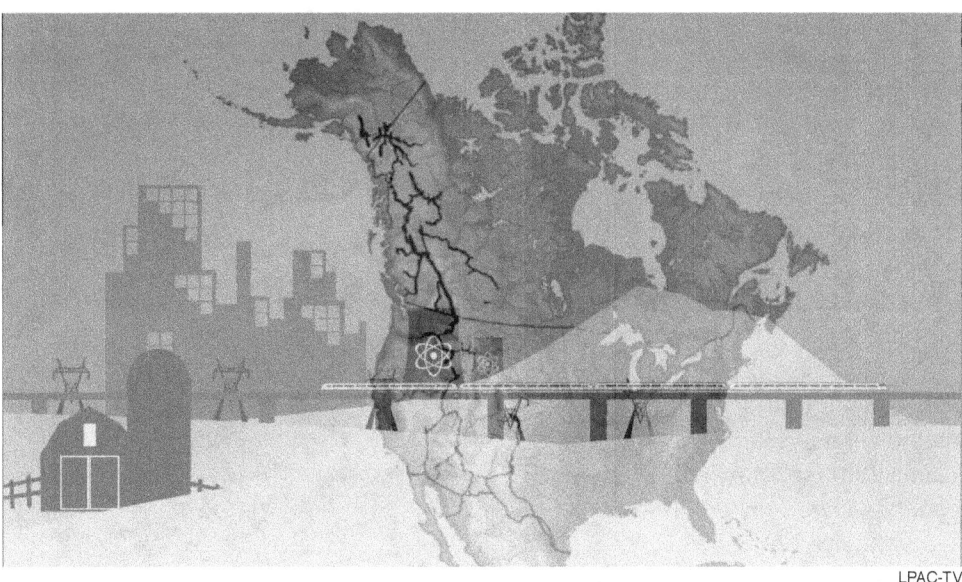

LPAC-TV

Rather than the term "infrastructure," LaRouche has introduced the term "platform," to describe an "upshift" of the Biosphere, produced by the application of the discovery of a universal physical princple. NAWAPA, as conceived by LaRouche and his scientific Basement team, represents such a platform. This image is taken from the LPAC-TV video, "NAWAPA, Water for Life" (http:// larouchepac.com/node/15576).

notion of the localized practice specific to some group of individuals within society.

The cross-over from the category of what may be treated as simply "platforms" as such, to the development of a society's potential and individual or local action, is to be located in the application of the discovery of a universal principle, such as a level of quality of practice of a body of physical science, or of Classical artistic composition and its performance. In short, we have the concept of the universal personality of a general population's productive potential, as one distinguished by the radiation of an efficiently valid discovery of some relatively higher, truly universal principle of physical science, or, equally, of Classical-artistic mode of composition.

In other words, we must distinguish between the general level of application of energy-flux density, and extraordinary higher, or lower cases within the same domain.

These, and comparable features of the environment on which human life of a certain level of quality depends, are comparable, in their effects, to the climate conditions near the surface of our planet. In the extreme case, these conditions are indispensable choices of feasible approaches both to the maintaining and developing of successively higher orders of organization of human life, within such bounds, this corresponds to the notion of the development of the conditions for not only life as such, but, that the level of productivity achievable is determined in ways aptly illustrated by the available quality of transport of human beings and their productivity.

It is to be emphasized, that among all species, only mankind is known to recreate its willfully adopted, specific behavior in ways which are to be compared, and contrasted to a higher "evolutionary" progress to a superior species of life within the animal kingdoms generally

LPAC-TV

The natural evolution of the conditions of life on Earth, is, in significant part, determined by qualitative shifts in the Solar system's relationship to our Galaxy. Shown: Our Solar system oscillates above and below the plane of the Milky Way, in a 60-million-year cycle.

To introduce this subject, let us refer, here, to the case of celebrated statesman Charlemagne's revolution in economy and culture, through integrating networks of inland transport of persons and freight through integrated networks of rivers and canals. This work effected under the leadership of Charlemagne, was one of the greatest leaps forward in the productive powers of labor presently known in the human species' European history. For an example from a later phase of European and North American progress, take the still higher "geopolitical" level of trans-continental rail and related transport. "Nuclear Age," or "Thermonuclear Age," typify relevant cases of qualitative leaps to higher, physical, "geopolitical" states of organization of society as a whole.

On Higher Physical Principles

To make clearer the significance of replacing the notion of "infrastructure" by "platforms," consider, once more, the profound changes in conditions for life-forms on this planet as Earth came into an oxygen-dominated phase, and the later shift to an "ozone" phase. We are challenged, presently, by two broad classifications of such phase-spaces. The one by the natural evolution of the conditions of life, as determined by qualitative shifts in the Solar system's relationship to our galaxy, and, within those bounds, the qualitative shifts in the

conditions for life within the bounds of the Solar system, and, within the Solar system, within the conditions for life-forms on Earth.

Following that, science must focus attention on those general changes in the potentiality of human habitation and development of our planet, which are willfully man-made principles of the environment in which mankind's habitation and work within human life and production, are brought to relatively higher stages of productivity, as within the newly created "level" of the potential representation by the environment. You should focus, first, on the strategic quality of logistical forms of "environmental factors" of quality of habitat and of facility of movement throughout the inhabited form of the developed environment.

To serve the purposes of this present phase of the discussion here and now, compare societies which are dominated by the strategic power represented by maritime movements, with the later, successive stages of approach, as through Charlemagne's development of an inland waterways system of combined rivers and connecting canals; then, proceed from that to the role of railways as supplements to riparian-canal systems, thence to trans-continental railways which represent a powerful, "geopolitical" challenge to imperial maritime capabilities.

The latter is the great issue which prompted the British Empire to drown the planet in a permanent state of global warfare from the time of the 1890 British ouster of Germany's Chancellor Bismarck through the ensuing state of virtually perpetual warfare throughout this planet since that time.

From there, move on to the fact, that since "World War II," we have had the prospect of a great change in the economy of life on this planet represented by the then-recent mastery of the domain of nuclear fission. We are now, for example, advancing toward general application of the higher cultural-physical phase of thermonuclear fusion, and beyond.

To bring about a relevant, competent understanding of the functional implications of such relatively primary kinds of logistical factors in government of mankind's habitation of our planet, we must take into account the broader and deeper implications of the concept of the "oligarchical principle" in shaping mankind's shaping of mankind's history. I shall classify this aspect of the problem by using the term "monkey business:" the role of cultures in which some people treat other people as, at best, virtually higher apes, rather than the human beings which they actually are.

Thus, there is the related issue of a functionally essential, strategic correlation, between the permission of some people to permit other people to use the higher forms of the principle of "fire," and the oligarchical model, in which latter case, a ruling class treats the lower classes of persons as virtually apes, denied the effective, willful choice of use of power, as such suppression of the conditions of life of the so-called "lower classes," is done in the name of "environmentalism" by the British monarchy and kindred nasty types today.

To summarize what I have reported in this present chapter of the report this far, that which I have chosen in order to arrive at an appropriate method of policy-shaping for a national economy, or a portion of technologically and culturally similar nations in the world economy, we must distinguish between the general "foundations" of the economy of a nation or related group of nations (what I have termed "the platforms"), and the way in which that foundation is utilized for the development of the local and regional applications of particular methods and capabilities of production represented by local production, services, and individual public and private enterprises.

To summarize this chapter's introductory remarks thus far, let us emphasize the level of scientific and cultural development of, on the one side, the foundations of the productive potential of a nation and its regions, and, on the other, the application of scientific and technological potential to planting and harvesting the fruits which depend upon the qualitative level of the general foundations on which the fruitfulness of the production throughout that region depends.

The Notion of Physical Principle

I think it preferable that I interrupt the line of the argument which I have been following within this chapter thus far, to bring into play the notion of a true universal physical principle, a notion which does not exist in the practice of either the crude "materialists," or either the Aristoteleans, nor the followers of the doctrine of "pleasure-pain" of such as Paolo Sarpi and the notoriously degraded Adam Smith.

So far in this present chapter, I have emphasized the use of fair descriptions, as if to "box in" principled conceptions, rather than address them more directly. Now, I must shift to direct representation.

In reality, there is no "space per se." There is no separation of "space" and "time," but, rather, there is an indivisibility of a space-time best fairly identified as "a space-time filled with cosmic radiation," a system of cosmic radiation which situates the "singularities" which a less sophisticated science prefers to identify as "particles" or the like.

That principled type of distinction has broad implications, but, here, I concentrate attention on one aspect.

The domain of the "cosmic radiation" of "space-time," can not be understood efficiently except for those cases in which the subject of primary interest is something which does not exist for either the followers of Aristotle or modern Sarpian Liberalism, to say little about the crudest form of sense-certainty. Since some of these implications pertaining to cosmic radiation are currently being addressed by a core grouping among my associates, I shall limit myself here to minimal considerations on this subject.

Expressed most simply, while avoiding actual error, the situation to be referenced here, is presented as follows.

No truly universal principle of nature can be deduced, in itself, as a derivative of a mathematical deduction. The most useful illustration of that point is the case of Albert Einstein's recognition of Johannes Kepler's uniquely original discovery of the principle of universal gravitation, as implying a universe which is finite, but not bounded. The proof of Einstein's conclusion on this account, is illustrated immediately by the method which Kepler employed to define a universal principle of gravitation, especially when one takes into account Kepler's method of experimental hypothesis for defining the principle of the Earth orbit. The construction of the duplication of the cube by Archytas, is an illustration of the case of a physical action which can not be represented deductively, but for which there is a construction.

This same principle is expressed systematically in the work of Bernhard Riemann, and, notably, the discoveries of the principles of the Biosphere and Noösphere by V.I. Vernadsky. Indeed, contrary to the hoax of Titius-Bode, every true discovery of a valid universal principle is literally metaphorical in the respect that its proof is not located within the domain of an extended notion of sense-perception.

The 15th-Century "Golden Renaissance" revived European civiliation following the 14th-Century "New Dark Age." Shown: "The Journey of the Magi," by Benozzo Gozzoli, 1459-61, a metaphor for the visit by leading scholars, statemen, and intellectuals, to the Council of Florence (1439).

Whereas, the universe is inherently creative, the creativity is not willfully generated in the way human creativity functions; it is the willful aspect of human creativity which distinguishes V.I. Vernadsky's Noösphere from the Biosphere. The role of the human intellect and its will in efficiently discovering successively higher orders of true creativity in the universe, is the essential distinction of man from beast.

Notably, the origin of new, valid expressions of creativity, is located in the domain corresponding to the Classical poetic method of metaphor, metaphor as a physically-experimentally anti-entropic, humanly willful discovery of what corresponds to a principle of the universe. Life itself is such a universal principle; human cognition as a principle, is a universal principle of a higher quality than life in itself. Such is the only valid meaning of the term "human creativity."

Mankind creates, and that willfully, specific types of higher states of organization in the universe than would be generated by other means. It is by such human activity, whether by some original inventor of the discovered principle, or by assimilating some broader implication of an already discovered such principle, that the essential changes of the human race to higher qualities of states of existence within the universe are accomplished in a willful mode.

The occurrence of such forms of human individual's such creativity has the characteristic of a change in the lawful ordering of the universe by the action of the human creative will. Man introduces a new state of lawfulness into the body of the universe, man, seen in Biblical terms of **Genesis** 1, as representative of man and woman "in the likeness of the creator," not in form, but in function.

The 'Golden Renaissance'

Consider the most crucial of the relevant developments of trans-Atlantic civilization during the period of accelerating emergence of a new kind of society which appeared at an accelerating rate throughout the early through middle decades of Europe's Fifteenth Century. Focus on the process leading into and beyond the mid-century's Florentine Renaissance—the so-called

"Golden Renaissance," and its expression as "the great ecumenical Council of Florence," a renaissance whose intellectual leadership featured, to most notable scientific and economic effect, the leading role of the figure soon to become known as Cardinal Nicholas of Cusa.

Divide the entire period into three principal parts, beginning since the earlier collapse of Fourteenth-century Europe into a so-called "New Dark Age," the process of a relevant discovery of civilization in Fifteenth Century Europe under the impact of the process culminating in the Florentine "Golden Renaissance," and the later descent into the 1492-1648 period of horrid religious warfare.

Nicholas of Cusa, the great "polymath" behind the ecumenical Council of Florence, is the founder of modern science.

To gain access to the "flavor" of the Fifteenth-century Renaissance itself, consider, in broad terms, situating that review among the crucial features of the developments in Europe during the Twelfth through Fourteenth centuries.

The close of the Tenth Century had seen the beginnings of a long wave of decline of the second phase of the Roman Empire, the Byzantine empire, and the rise of Venice as the center of the leading, imperial form of monetary power in Europe generally. The character of the opening of this period, is identified by the rising role of Venice as the monetarist power of Europe, and the expression of that character of the period by the Norman Conquest of the British Isles and the process of the Crusades, leading into the mass-murderous "New Dark Age" of the Fourteenth Century.

That Fourteenth-century "New Dark Age," is to be remembered, since the so-called "Norman Conquest," as the period of the notorious Hildebrand, a period dominated by evil Crusades, such as the Norman Conquest itself, warfare launched under rising Venetian monetarist financing and manipulations. It was a period which, from the time of the Norman Conquest into the depths of the Fourteenth-century "New Dark Age," a period of broadly chaotic, genocidal nightmares, leading into that vastly and stubbornly genocidal nightmare, a horror which began to end only with the cleansing of a Christian church deeply corrupted by its Venetian direction, until the rising contrary developments, known as the Renaissance, during the early through middle of the Fifteenth Century.

Return to touch on some matters to which I have referred earlier in this chapter.

Cardinal Nicholas of Cusa

The modern expression of this notion of actual, universal physical principles was introduced to the "post-dark-age" developments in Fifteenth-century Europe around the rallying point of what I have already identified here as the great ecumenical Council of Florence. Many from that time contributed to this, including, notably, the Jeanne d'Arc whose specific intention and heroism inspired the great Councils of the Christian Church through the middle of that century. The most fertile of those minds engaged in launching the Fifteenth-century Florentine-centered European Renaissance, was what I have already referenced as the great "polymath" of the period, Cardinal Nicholas of Cusa.

There were two outstanding historical figures of the period leading into the Great Ecumenical Council of Florence, Jeanne d'Arc, who was baked alive by the English (Norman) inquisition, but whose role and its reflexes on Europe not only bestirred the councils of the Christian church during that time, but which had a crucial effect in shaping the history of Europe from that time on, through the great role of France's King Louis XI. This was the same Louis XI whose role inspired the revolution in England led by Henry VII.

These developments, sparked in significant degree by Cusa's **Concordantia Catholica** defining the modern sovereign nation-state, and Cusa's formal founding of modern physical science, his **De Docta Ignorantia**, remain outstanding, still throughout the world today, as the root of the launching of all competent strains of modern physical science today.

For example, it was Christopher Columbus' reading

of the legacy of Nicholas of Cusa, in Cusa's proposal to build up civilization by trans-oceanic voyages to distant continents, which prompted Columbus and others to cross the Atlantic, as a measure to save European civilization from the effects of a fresh Venetian launching of a European dark age of wars and the like. It was Cusa's initiatives in the founding of modern science which were chiefly responsible for every great scientific figure of Europe from the late Fifteenth, Sixteenth, and Seventeenth centuries, with strong reverberations among all competent currents of fundamental scientific progress. Such as Bernhard Riemann, Max Planck, and Albert Einstein, to this day.

As the case of Cusa exemplifies this, all great movements in physical science were essentially "polymathic," as for the great, avowed follower of Johannes Kepler, Gottfried Leibniz, for whom there was never any separation of the world-outlooks of Classical artistic composition and physical science.

Thus, the mid-Fifteenth-century great ecumenical Council of Florence, was that true Renaissance of European civilization on which all of the good developments in European civilization have depended for their adopted roots, to the present day.

It was not the entry into Paradise; it was an entirely original quality of advance in mankind's insight into mankind, which emerged to remain, thus far, an imperilled new force of civilization on which the creation and usually imperilled existence of our United States has depended up through the presently, monstrously imperilled United States of America today.

Many from that period of the Renaissance contributed significantly to this greatest of all known qualitative achievements of mankind to the present day, including the rise of the Federal Republic of the United States out of the seedlings planted in Massachusetts during the middle of the Seventeenth Century. That subject, so situated as I have done immediately above, is the kernel of the argument which I present here and now.

'The Massachusetts Syndrome'

In this present report, up to this present point in my account, I have emphasized the physical accomplishments which supplied the foundations of all European society since the appearance of the roots of the influence of Solon of Athens. Now, bearing in mind my preceding remarks, we are obliged to shift our point of view in a qualitative way.

Up to the beginning of the present chapter of this report, I had emphasized the physical principles of progress, as such. Now, we must shift from emphasis on the commonplace, narrower, more popular notions of physical effects, to the role of human culture in generating the causes for those leaps in the quality of life on this planet which have been fruits of what we call "culture."

By "culture," I now signify the transformation of the physical quality of the existence of our human species on which the physical fate of human life on this planet absolutely depends; I mean to emphasize the role of the cultural impact of the Fifteenth-century, Florentine-centered "Renaissance" in producing what became the Seventeenth-century high point of the Massachusetts Bay Colony under the leadership of the Winthrops and Mathers, and of what survived of the great Massachusetts Renaissance in trans-Atlantic civilization, to become the heritage of the Eighteenth Century's Benjamin Franklin, that heritage of our United States, which is expressed by the American Revolution and by the launching of the constitutional, anti-monetarist credit-system which is to be recognized as the United States.

So, turn to the second of the two approaches which I have outlined for this chapter of the report. Take the model historical case of the original foundation and development of the Massachusetts Bay Colony prior to both the last period of suppression of the colony's development, a period of peril during the reign of England's James II, and the crushing of the colony following the accession of that "New Venetian Party" which was led into power in the British Isles by William of Orange.

To understand the roots of our American Revolution, we must take into account, and emphasize, what is presently the almost unknown concept of what is truly a universal physical principle. This is a notion of principle which does not exist in the imagination of such as the followers of the ancient Aristotle or the modern Paolo Sarpi, the true notion of a discoverable, universal physical principle.

In notable degree, that Renaissance in science and the principles of humanism, was brought into modern European culture as an echo of the process leading into the great achievements of Plato and his associate, that Pythagorean, Archytas of Tarentum, whose signal

"The great obstacle to human reason has been the popular delusion of belief in 'sense-certainty,'" LaRouche writes. As the great conductor Wilhelm Furtwängler warned, "music requires its performance 'between the notes.'" Shown: Furtwängler, conducting, in the 1930s.

achievement had been, what the later Eratosthenes underscored as the method of construction required for the duplication of the cube.

The Human Mind

The great obstacle to human reason has been the popular delusion of belief in "sense-certainty." The worst form of that delusion, has been the presumption that the evidence of each of the given senses has an independent authority of its own, and that that authority defines what the mind should adopt as if with a cry tantamount to "that settles it!"

My own views on sense-perception were settled for me by early 1953, when I adopted the implications of the Third Section of Bernhard Riemann's 1854 habilitation dissertation, in which Riemann develops his famous argument against the foolish presumption that

mathematics, such as that pathetic mewling called statistics, defines physical science. Our sense-functions are not merely the equivalent of a set of sense-organs, but, nonetheless, they provide us, not with reality, but with something akin to the shadows cast by an unseeable reality. Thus, there could be no decent poetry which is not premised on the principle of enunciated irony which is typified in the tendency for metaphor. As the great conductor Furtwängler warned, music requires its performance "between the notes."

What we can properly claim that we know, is the discovery of universal principles, as Archytas crafted the duplication of the cube, and as Johannes Kepler defined, uniquely, and with perfect originality, the principle of universal gravitation.

Consider the great lesson provided by Classical poetry, uttered accordingly.

The function of the great principle of metaphor, as in Classical poetry, and as in musical counterpoint composed and performed according to the principle of Johann Sebastian Bach, is to provide mankind with a prescience of the approach of a discovery of a great principle. We call this "Classical artistic" composition, because it is presented to us as if a voice of truth spoken from the future, not yet the present. It is the shadow cast by a principle of the universe which is yet to be spoken; thus, properly uttered, or performed as music, it is the idea which can never be deduced, since it is the prescience of that reality which is still waiting impatiently to become discovered.

Those who do not serve that principle, should—please—never compose Classical poetry or music. All competent practice of scientific discovery depends upon exactly that same principle of the prescience of a hand from the future reaching in to touch one's soul with a discovered principle of nature yet to be born. The true mission of the human individual is to feel the prescience of the principle which is about to be born.

Such is the true content of the much-abused word named for a prescience of immortality, a prescience which you might wish to call "love" of being, in that moment, truly human.

EDITORIAL

Why the U.S., Russia, China, India and Germany Must Overcome Geopolitics!

by Helga Zepp-LaRouche, chairwoman of the
German political party Civil Rights Movement Solidarity (BüSo)

Jan. 27—The world is indeed out of joint. But one thing is certain: The current array of crises will not be resolved with old formulas, and certainly not with geopolitical gambits, color revolutions à la George Soros, or the Old Testament "eye for an eye" approach of the perhaps not-so-liberal publisher-editor of *Die Zeit* Josef Joffe. What is required instead is a higher level of reason, which identifies the common interests of all the world's nations. Precisely this level of thinking was expressed by Russian Foreign Minister Sergei Lavrov in his Jan. 25 speech before the Duma, in which he proposed an alliance among Washington, Moscow, and Beijing to find solutions for today's challenges.

In a variation on Schiller's poem, "The Commencement of the New Century," one is tempted to say: "Two mighty systems strive for undivided mastery of the world"—namely, the old, war-inducing system of geopolitics, and the new, future-oriented paradigm of the common destiny of mankind. The representatives of the first of these—the collapsing, formerly neoliberal order of globalization (*laissez-faire* economic liberalism)—are reacting to their perceived loss of power with verbal outbursts appropriately diagnosed as clinical hysteria. But in this camp, there is apparently little honor among thieves, or various factions. The best example is British Prime Minister Theresa May's visit to Washington, during which she tried to corral the new U.S. administration into the geometry of the British Empire. The new order, on the contrary, is guided by entirely opposite principles, based on the win-win cooperation of China's New Silk Road, which is rapidly expanding.

Lavrov's Proposal

In this respect, Sergei Lavrov's intervention was of the highest importance: "We believe that as Russia, the United States, and China build their relations, this tri-angle should not be closed or directed towards some projects that could worry other states. [They should be] open and fair. I am convinced that the economic structure of Russia, the United States, and China is such that there is a great deal of complementarity in the material and economic sphere." These three nations can also splay an important role with respect to international security questions, he said. Russia and China are already cooperating well in this area, and they expect that President Donald Trump, who has already stated that the United States will no longer interfere in the internal affairs of other nations, will cooperate as well.

The spokeswoman for the Chinese Foreign Ministry, Hua Chunying, immediately supported the Russian proposal for trilateral cooperation among these three nations, which are "leading global powers" as well as permanent members of the UN Security Council. They have "great responsibility for global peace, stability, and development," she said.

Should Donald Trump opt for close cooperation with Russia, China, and India, that would, in fact, spell the end of geopolitics. Fear of such an outcome obviously motivated British Prime Minister May's visit to Trump—the first foreign head of government to visit—where she then endlessly rhapsodized about the wonderful relationship between Margaret Thatcher and President Reagan, which "made the modern world." This Anglo-American special relationship must again assume leadership for the new century, she said.

The *London Times* suggested that May does not underestimate Trump, but should "tap" the spirit which led to Brexit, as the most important ideological bridge to Trump's White House. The *Financial Times* fantasized about an additional intention of May's visit, namely, to exploit this special relationship in order to split Russia from China through various concessions and manipulations. The *New York Times*, for its part, titled its article, "British Alignment with Trump Threatens European Order," alluding to Trump's negative attitude toward the European Union (EU).

The total denial of reality by the supporters of geopolitics is producing ludicrous effects. For example, Joffe argues against Trump's protectionist measures by saying that globalization has "created fabulous wealth which supports the magnanimous social state and creates a cushion for the losers. Protectionism benefits favored industries, but allows the country to become poorer—its weakest classes, first of all."

This is the classic *laissez faire* narrative, which says it is wonderful that the profiteers of the casino economy become fabulously rich, then bestow charity on the poor, and thus ennoble themselves. It is precisely that narrow-minded stupidity which the Brexit, Trump's election, and the no vote in the Italian constitutional referendum rejected.

Joffe's conclusion that Europe must take over the role of the United States "to save the liberal world order," is just as ludicrous as the question posed by the daily *Die Welt*: "Will Chancellor Merkel Become the Counterpart to President Trump and the Leader of the Free West?" Norbert Röttgen, chairman of the *Bundestag* Committee on Foreign Affairs, has similar ambitions for himself, and indulges in one media highlight after another. He wants to confront Trump with "new social alliances" and is apparently placing his hope in people like Sen. John McCain.

The Four Basic Economic Laws

There is only one sure way to overcome the strategic confusion outlined here: The common interests of all the world's nations must be established on a higher plane—a plane at which the purported contradictions disappear. The four basic economic laws which Lyndon LaRouche has identified for overcoming the crisis, provide the basis for achieving it:

• The first, indispensable measure must be to avert the threatened crash of the transatlantic financial system—which threatens to be worse than that of 2008— by reinstating the Glass-Steagall banking separation law. Under the leadership of the LaRouche Political Action Committee (LPAC), many organizations in the United States are mobilizing to escalate the pressure on President Trump to keep this campaign promise, and re-introduce Glass-Steagall in the form of its 1933 original, in his Feb. 28 State of the Union address, at the latest.

• Second, a National Bank in the tradition of Alexander Hamilton must be created, whose sole aim must be to finance infrastructure, industry, and basic scientific research according to the strict principles of physical economy—which means raising the productivity of labor and industrial capacity, and thus producing full employment.

• Third, an international credit system must facilitate long-term international cooperation for the reconstruction of the world economy according to the same principles as above.

• Fourth, there must be international cooperation on a crash program to achieve nuclear fusion, which would give mankind energy and raw materials security, and to establish through space exploration the future-oriented, higher plane, which is needed to create an actual order of peace among nations.

If Trump accepts Lavrov's offer and constructive cooperation among the United States, Russia, and China is implemented, such win-win cooperation is also within reach of all nations. The first contacts between Trump and Indian Prime Minister Narendra Modi have already led to positive declarations of intent.

Under these circumstances, Germany must associate itself with this new strategic alliance. It is in our most fundamental interest to cooperate with the United States, Russia, China, India, and many other countries in the economic development of the Near and Middle East, and to take up the long neglected mission of industrializing Africa. Only in this way will the refugee crisis be resolved in a humane way and will we be able, at least partially, to make amends for having allowed ourselves to sit back and watch the aggressive wars of Bush, Obama, Blair, and Cameron in the Middle East without doing anything—or rather, for having allowed the European governments to indirectly or partially to support these wars.

German Foreign Minister Frank-Walter Steinmeier was correct in his observation that, with Trump's election, the old order of the 20th Century is gone once and for all. And that is a very good thing. It is now up to us to ensure that the new order will respect the true identity of mankind as a creative species—in that we concentrate on those great challenges which we are the only living species capable of meeting. Among these challenges are such questions as the discovery of the characteristic or nature of life itself, the role of human creativity in the universe, and the principle of development of the universe, which, according to our current understanding, consists of something like two trillion galaxies. And, last but not least, the question of realizing in the individual a beautiful character with the aid of aesthetic education.